Cricket Made Simple

Ann Waterhouse

CRICKET
Made Simple

An Entertaining Introduction to the Game
for Mums & Dads
Illustrations by Amanda Stiby Harris

Meyer & Meyer Sport

British Library Cataloguing in Publication Data
A catalogue record for this book is available from the British Library

Cricket Made Simple
Maidenhead: Meyer & Meyer Sport (UK) Ltd., 2016
ISBN 978-1-78255-079-2
Previously published as *Sue Porter's Guide to Cricket* in 2013 by Ann M Waterhouse Ltd.

Aachen, Auckland, Beirut, Cairo, Cape Town, Dubai, Hägendorf, Hong Kong, Indianapolis, Manila, New Delhi, Singapore, Sydney, Teheran, Vienna

 Member of the World Sport Publishers' Association (WSPA)

Manufacturing: Print Consult GmbH, Germany, Munich
ISBN 978-1-78255-079-2
E-Mail: info@m-m-sports.com
www.m-m-sports.com

Dedication

This book is dedicated to that hardy band of supporters: mothers, fathers, partners and grandparents who bravely sit outside in what is euphemistically known as 'summer' in the British Isles, to support their youngsters or partners as they play the totally baffling game that is . . . cricket.

As the final book in our trilogy, this book is also dedicated to artist, sculptor and illustrator Amanda Stiby Harris who sadly passed away in June 2015 just before this book was completed for publication. This series of books would have been far less entertaining without her input and the author will always be grateful for her support and assistance in their preparation.

Contents

Acknowledgements

The author would like to thank the following for their assistance in bringing this book to the reader:

Caterham School, where she watched her young sons learn the game of cricket and without whose support her original book would never have been written, especially John Moulton, former House Master at Caterham School and cricket umpire, whose early advice ensured the accuracy of the information contained in both this and our previous books.

Zoe Chambers and Daphne Sales, without whom the author's knowledge of a cricketing mother's life would not have been complete.

Geoff Knight, for his invaluable help in reviewing the revision in 2013, to ensure all the latest developments in the game were captured for the new supporter.

And last, but never least, my late father, without whom my interest in cricket would never have been kindled in the first place, and my sons Gareth and Alan, for giving me a reason to sit by boundaries and learn to love this great British game. I would especially like to thank my husband David whose support throughout the process of preparing all three books has been unwavering. I can honestly say I couldn't have done it without his help and support.

Introduction

'Keep your bat and pad together, Jenkinson, I'm sure your father isn't paying nine thousand pounds a term to have you flashing at balls outside the off stump. What do you mean, "it hurt"? Of course it hurt, it's a cricket ball, it's supposed to hurt!'

Many of you picking up this small tome will wonder why anyone would choose to play a game that requires them to wear protective padding all over their legs, hands, arms and head; is played with a ball that really hurts if it hits them hard (which it frequently will) and also requires them to stand out in the open air regardless of the temperature for most of the daylight hours, frequently without a clear result to either side.

I just hope if your son or daughter (or perhaps your boyfriend or girlfriend) has persuaded you to come along and watch them play, this little book will give you a bit more of an idea of what is going on and help you gain greater enjoyment from watching matches in the future.

If you're a young cricketer, just learning the ropes in your first season, you might also find some of the information I provide useful: placing a field; what kit to use and how to care for your kit – all this is covered at some point in this book. If nothing else I hope you'll be amused by my take on this wonderful game.

Throughout the book you will find website references and we have provided the full links to these at the back of the book. The web links are also available on our website:

» www.sueportersguide.com

So just what is cricket?

Hopefully you will have already seen cricket in some form or other, either on television, at a school playing field or in a local park. The pundits tell us it is synonymous with the sound of leather on willow and hot summer's days spent relaxing in the semi-rural atmosphere of a cricket ground, but for the purposes of this book, let's assume that you actually know nothing whatsoever about the game.

For many cricketing supporters it will always be remembered for freezing temperatures, pouring rain, damp sandwiches, tepid tea and hours and hours of sitting, just waiting for something exciting to happen.

You may recognise some of the famous names from the cricketing world, Ian Botham, Freddie Flintoff, Shane Warne, Alistair Cook et al. If you already have some understanding I apologise for the introductory detail but hope you will find something to amuse or enlighten you on these pages.

Back in the 1970s, some wag produced an explanation of first-class cricket for foreigners, that ran:

You have two sides, one out in the field and one in.

Each man that's in the side that's in goes out, and when he's out he comes in and the next man goes in until he's out.

When they are all out, the side that's out comes in and the side that's been in goes out and tries to get those coming in, out.

Sometimes you get men still in and not out.

When a man goes out to go in, the men who are out try to get him out, and when he is out he goes in and the next man in goes out and goes in.

There are two men called umpires who stay out all the time and they decide when the men who are in are out.

> When both sides have been in and all the men have been out, and both sides have been out twice after all the men have been in, including those who are not out, that is the end of the game!

Confused? You may well be, but hopefully I'll be able to clarify at least some of this explanation in the pages that follow. I certainly hope that my small book will provide a better explanation for anyone new to the game of cricket, and I will do my best to make the information really easy to understand.

An apology

Cricket has been played in some form or other by both men and women since the 14th century, and the game is played to a very high standard by girls and women in the 21st century. Indeed the number of girls and women playing has doubled in the last few years and there are currently over 700,000 playing regularly across the UK alone.

However, much of this book describes boys' and men's cricket and I apologise if the girls feel I don't pay sufficient attention to their role in the current game. Rest assured that no slight is intended, it's just that my level of expertise lies in supporting fathers, boyfriends, husbands and sons rather than mothers, wives, girlfriends and daughters. The information I provide will apply equally to both sexes playing the game, so I hope you can mentally convert *he* to *she* and *him* to *her* whenever you need to. I have tried to include the fairer sex in my descriptions on a regular basis, but I can also quote from the *Spirit of the Game* that is now enshrined within cricket's laws:

'The use, throughout the text, of pronouns indicating the male gender is purely for brevity. Except where specifically stated otherwise [this book] is to be read as applying to women and girls equally as to men and boys.'

Cricket made simple

So here we go with our guide for new supporters and spectators. According to Wikipedia (the modern equivalent of the philosopher's stone) 'cricket is a bat-and-ball game played between two teams of 11 players on a field, at the centre of which is a rectangular 22-yard long pitch. One team bats, trying to score as many runs as possible, while the other team bowls and fields, trying to dismiss the batsmen and thus limit the runs scored by the batting team. A run is scored by the striking batsman hitting the ball with his bat, running to the opposite end of the pitch and touching it down behind the crease without being dismissed. The teams switch between batting and fielding at the end of an innings.' A simple and in some ways quite detailed description, but still probably as clear as mud to anyone who has never played the game.

I can add, as my basic introduction, that cricket is a game of skill and strategy played between two teams of players. Each team takes its turn to bat and score runs while the other team bowls and fields and tries to dismiss the batsmen. Each turn is called an innings.

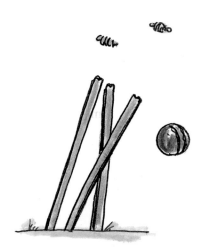

If at any time in the book you feel you want more detail than I have supplied, I can certainly recommend the BBC's online sports information and Wikipedia, as well as the traditional cricket websites of the Marylebone Cricket Club (MCC), England and Wales Cricket Board (ECB) and the International Cricket Council (ICC). You'll find website links to several useful sites at the back of the book.

Before I head off into the details, I'd like to start with some cricketing history to set the scene for you.

A cricket history lesson

Researching the history of cricket has proved to be somewhat baffling, with lots of differing ideas on the origins of the game. I have, however, done my best to pull the basic facts from a myriad collection of sources and hope they are as accurate as possible.

The game is generally believed to have originated in England among shepherds using their crooks as bats, and the earliest wickets may well have been narrow sheep pens. There are also pictures in existence of women playing a game like cricket as early as the 1300s. The earliest men's games that were officially recorded (interestingly from law court records) were played in southeast England in the 1550s. Initially a single wicket was used, as it still is in ancient games like stoolball that continue to be played in southern England.

Originally bats were curved, rather like hockey sticks or clubs. Straight bats were only introduced in about 1780, as initially all bowling was underarm and until the 1760s the ball was merely rolled or skimmed along the ground to the batsman. After this it was pitched and finally from the 19th century players bowled as they do today. Initially this was done with a round arm action but then the modern overarm bowling technique was developed. It was these changes that led to the introduction of the straight bat to cope with the now bouncing ball.

The structure of the ball was also fixed around this time. It was traditionally made of cork covered with red leather. The most popular ball now describes itself as being 'a superb quality hand stitched 4-piece construction with a 5-layer quilted centre. Waxed and finished and with a cover made from selected first grade alum tanned steer hide with fine linen stitching.' Making a modern cricket ball requires great skill and dexterity and the construction remains extremely complicated to this day.

There are many other interesting and indeed curious suggestions for the beginnings of cricket. There is a picture which is kept in the Bodleian Library in Oxford, depicting mediaeval monks playing a game in a field. One brother is bowling to another who is attempting to hit the ball with his cricce (a staff or crutch). This is thought by experts to be a game of 'club-ball', a forerunner of cricket, but it could of course simply be a picture of some monks having a bit of a laugh in the middle of a field! Certainly academics are divided even on the derivation of the word *cricket*, some thinking it Saxon, and some determined that both the word and the game itself are Flemish.

The history of cricket matches is kept by Wisden, the chronicler of the game, whose annual almanac gives details of cricketing records and the results of all matches played. Published every year since 1864, the latest edition contains coverage of every first-class game in every cricket-playing nation and gives reports and scorecards for all Tests matches and one-day internationals too.

The birthplace of modern competitive or professional cricket is generally agreed to be the Hambledon Club in Hampshire. Some of that club's members went on to form the White Conduit Club in London in the mid-1780s and this then changed its name over time to become the Marylebone Cricket Club (MCC). It all started when the club's groundsman, Thomas Lord, laid the first club ground in Dorset Square in London. Subsequent movements of that turf by Thomas Lord finally resulted in the establishment of Lord's Cricket Ground in St John's Wood

in northwest London, which is the current home of the MCC, and also Middlesex County Cricket Club.

In Thomas Lord's time the pitch was prepared before a match by allowing sheep to come in and graze on the grass. However in the mid-1800s the club acquired its first mechanical mowing machine and then appointed its first official groundsman in 1864.

The first recorded match played by women took place at Gosden Common, Surrey, on 26th July 1745. Around 1807, a lady cricketer named Christina Willes is said to have introduced the round arm bowling style – thought to have been necessary to avoid catching her bowling hand on her skirts! So the ladies have had a major influence on the development of the game since its early days and the first official club for women, the White Heather Club, was formed in 1887.

The early laws of cricket were pretty basic and included the prescribed length of the pitch (22 yards), the use of two stumps (just one at each end of the pitch), underarm bowling and four balls to an over.

These days there are 42 laws (a number that has remained constant for some time despite a major review in 2000 – more on this later). Most have clauses and sub-clauses within them and they cover such matters as time wasting; umpires; substitutes; the rolling, sweeping, mowing, watering and marking of the pitch; the tea interval (a vital element for all cricketing supporters); dead balls and unfair play. The laws are readily available online at

» http://www.lords.org/mcc/laws-of-cricket/

They remain a serious guide to how the game should be played, running to over 150 pages of detailed guidance and instruction. Indeed the MCC now includes a detailed question-and-answer section for players or officials who wish to check any aspects of the laws. Within the online edition you will find videos explaining details of the laws, so there's no excuse for not knowing the laws these days.

I can't describe the history of cricket without introducing you to The Ashes, the Test cricket series that has been played between England and Australia since 1882. It is one of the most celebrated rivalries in international sport and it is currently played biennially, at alternating venues in England and Australia. It is named after a satirical newspaper obituary article published in *The Sporting Times* in 1882 on the occasion of the first loss to Australia on English soil. The obituary stated:

In affectionate remembrance of

ENGLISH CRICKET,
WHICH DIED AT THE OVAL

ON

29th AUGUST, 1882,

Deeply lamented by a large circle of sorrowing
friends and acquaintances.

R.I.P.
N.B. The body will be cremated and the ashes taken to Australia.

The English media then dubbed the next tour to Australia (UK winter 1882–83) as the quest to 'regain The Ashes', and so the story continued. During that 1882-83 tour to Australia, the then England captain, one Ivo Bligh, was presented with a small terracotta urn containing ashes as a memento of the tour, which England won. The ashes are thought to be the remains of a bail ceremonially burned to create them. Considered a personal gift by Bligh, the urn was eventually donated to the MCC by his widow, and it remains in their museum to this day. Replicas of the urn are often raised in celebration of a victory of The Ashes Test series, but the actual urn is never used in this way.

As is often the case in cricket history, the story of The Ashes urn is full of contradictions, but this is the generally agreed version. There are many excellent books and websites on the subject of cricket history (see the links pages at the end of this book) and if your interest has been kindled by this book, do search them out in your local library, bookshop or online.

Cricket is popular across the planet. Having started out in former British Empire countries such as Australasia, the Indian subcontinent, the West Indies and southern Africa, it is now played right around the world. See the table below showing all the members of the ICC in 2015.

Member-ship	Africa (22)	Americas (17)	Asia (22)	East Asia-Pacific (11)	Europe (33)
Full members (10)	South Africa	West Indies	Bangladesh	Australia	England
	Zimbabwe		India	New Zealand	
			Pakistan		
			Sri Lanka		

Member-ship	Africa (22)	Americas (17)	Asia (22)	East Asia-Pacific (11)	Europe (33)
Associate members (38)	Botswana	Argentina	Afghanistan	Fiji	Belgium
	Kenya	Bermuda	Hong Kong	Japan	Denmark
	Namibia	Canada	Kuwait	Papua New Guinea	France
	Nigeria	Cayman Islands	Malaysia	Vanuatu	Germany
	Tanzania	Suriname	Nepal		Gibraltar
	Uganda	USA	Oman		Guernsey
	Zambia		Singapore		Ireland
			Thailand		Israel
			United Arab Emirates		Jersey
					Netherlands
					Scotland
Affiliate members (57)	Cameroon	Bahamas	Bahrain	Cook Islands	Austria
	Gambia	Belize	Bhutan	Indonesia	Bulgaria
	Ghana	Brazil	Brunei	Philippines	Croatia

Member-ship	Africa (22)	Americas (17)	Asia (22)	East Asia-Pacific (11)	Europe (33)
Affiliate members (57)	Lesotho	Chile	China	Samoa	Cyprus
	Malawi	Costa Rica	Iran	South Korea	Czech Republic
	Mali	Falkland Islands	Maldives		Estonia
	Morocco	Mexico	Myanmar		Finland
	Mozambique	Panama	Qatar		Greece
	Rwanda	Peru	Saudi Arabia		Hungary
	Seychelles	Turks & Caicos Islands			Isle of Man
	Sierra Leone				Luxembourg
	St Helena				Malta
	Swaziland				Norway
					Portugal
					Romania
					Russia
					Slovenia
					Spain

Member-ship	Africa (22)	Americas (17)	Asia (22)	East Asia-Pacific (11)	Europe (33)
					Sweden
					Turkey

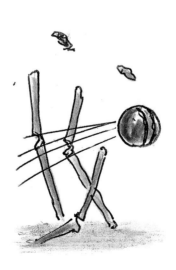

Terminology for beginners

Before getting into more details of the game itself, here are a few words and phrases that you will come across in this book, whose explanation early on might make the subsequent text slightly easier to understand. The list is not comprehensive and there will be some terms that we'll explain later in the book, but I hope it will help you get started on your pathway of discovery. You will find a link to a full online cricket glossary at the end of the book.

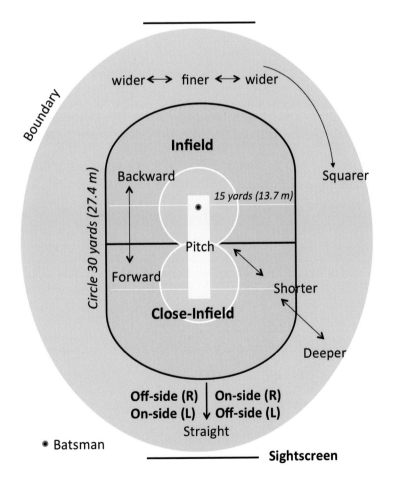

The Playing Area

Bail(s)	Small moulded sticks placed on top of stumps at the beginning of a match; one, or both, of which need to be dislodged for a batsmen to be out bowled, stumped, run out or hit wicket.
Boundary	The edge of the playing area, usually marked by a white line, rope or low fence. Also the description applied to a ball that crosses the field boundary and scores four runs.
Close infield	The area of the cricket ground closest to the pitch (see the basic diagram of a cricket ground on the previous page).
Crease	The crease is officially defined as the back or inside edge of the crease markings. These white lines mark the area in front of the wickets in which a batsman may safely bat and within which a bowler must bowl to avoid his delivery of the ball being deemed a no-ball (see the plan of a pitch on the next page). These marks include the popping or batting crease, the bowling crease and the return crease.
Infield	The area of the field closest to the pitch.
Net(s)	An area of the cricket ground set aside for practice, with high netting surrounding the pitches to allow batsmen and bowlers to practice without having to chase the balls all over the field. Some nets are in fixed areas at the edge of the cricket ground. Others are portable nets that are put up over a pitch marked on the ground whenever a practice session is needed. This is common on large county grounds.
Outfield	That part of the field of play between the square and the boundary edge.

The Playing Area

Pitch

The 22-yard (20.12 m) strip between the two wickets, ten feet (3.05 m) in width, being defined as five feet either side of an imaginary line joining the two middle stumps. Large county grounds will have several pitches marked out and will switch between them from match to match, using several pitches over the course of a season.

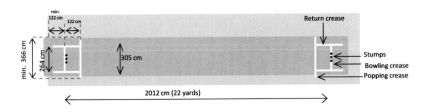

Sight screen(s)

Two large – usually wooden – screens on wheels placed at either end of the field in line with the pitch. Painted white, they are designed to give the batsman a better view of the incoming ball once it has been bowled and are always positioned behind the bowler's line of delivery. As larger cricket grounds may have several pitches marked out on them, the screens have to be moveable, hence the wheels.

The screens at county grounds are often made up of moving slats that can be rotated to display different sides. One side of the sight screen construction will be plain white, one plain black and up to two more sides can be printed with advertisements. During Twenty20 matches played at night, where a white ball is used, the black version enables the batsman to see the white ball easier in the more difficult lighting conditions of a day/night game.

See the supporters' etiquette section on page 125 for reasons to avoid sitting in front of or near this important piece of equipment.

The Playing Area	
Square	The area mowed around the pitch to define a specially prepared part of playing area. Usually a rectangular shape on most cricket pitches.
Stump(s)	The three long wooden sticks with a groove in the top and spikes on the bottom which, together with the bails, form a wicket. One set is placed at each end of the pitch as shown on the diagram on the previous page.
Wicket(s)	The three stumps and bails together.

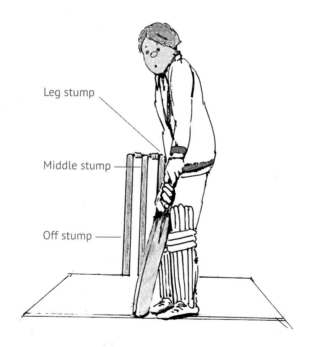

Leg stump

Middle stump

Off stump

Equipment	
Arm pad or forearm guard	A pad that straps to the forearm to protect the bones from damage whilst batting (see later in this section for more details on external protective equipment).
Bat	Traditionally made of willow and consisting of a blade with shoulder, handle and grip. Curiously this piece of equipment requires some effort on the part of the owner to make it fully usable, including oiling and knocking-in (see the kit care section on page 116 for full details). In terms of the laws, the definition of the bat also includes the hand(s) holding the bat and any part of the glove(s) on those hands.
Boots	Traditionally made of white leather with a strengthened toe cap and metal studs embedded in the sole (see the section on purchasing kit on page 67 for more detail). Also known as cricket shoes.
Box	The plastic or metal protective device for insertion in a pouch or specially designed briefs worn by men and boys to protect sensitive organs against damage from bat or ball. Also known as the groin protector.
Cap	A hat worn by cricketers to protect them from the sun. Caps are also awarded in special circumstances to outstanding players at school and senior levels. International players are described as being capped when they play for their country.
Colours	A tie or other insignia awarded to members of a house, club or school team when they have played particularly well during a cricket season.

Equipment	
External protective equipment	This is any visible item of apparel worn for protection against external blows. For a batsman, items permitted are a protective helmet, external leg guards (batting pads), batting gloves and, if visible, forearm guards or arm pads. For a fielder, only a protective helmet is permitted, except in the case of a wicket-keeper, for whom wicket-keeping pads and gloves are also permitted.
Gloves	Padded and specially designed to protect the batsmen's hands from damage. Special gloves are used by wicket-keepers with webbing between the first finger and thumb, to aid them in catching the ball. All the other fielders in a team play without gloves.
Helmet	The protective headgear needed to protect skulls from the marauding effects of very fast bowling. Originally worn at senior level only, helmets are now available for the novice cricketer too, and indeed current ECB directives make this headgear mandatory for all young batsmen facing fast bowlers, as well as young wicket-keepers and fielders standing close to the stumps.

Equipment	
Leg pads	Protective leg pads are worn by all batsmen and the wicket-keeper. Wicket-keepers have special pads which differ from the leg pads used by batsmen. Close fielders frequently wear shin protecting pads too but these must be worn under their clothing.
Hidden pads, including thigh and chest pads	Batsmen can also wear inner and outer thigh pads, which come in specially designed fitted shorts. In addition, there are chest pads and a bewildering array of options for the new player to contemplate if they wish to protect themselves from the effects of being hit by the ball.

Players and Personnel	
Batsmen	Two at a time. In an ideal world the batsman facing the bowler hits the ball every time it is bowled correctly at him, whilst avoiding being caught and protecting his wicket; however it is the bowler's job to ensure that he cannot do this and to try to dismiss him (i.e. get him out). A batsman is described as being on strike when facing the bowler.
Bowlers	One at a time from the two ends of the pitch. Ideally the bowler would like to hit the wicket with every ball he bowls. Obviously this is never the case in reality, or else matches would be over extremely rapidly. Some balls are bowled specifically to tempt the batsman into hitting out in such a way that he will give a catch to the fielders, and get out caught.
Chinaman	No, not a resident of China, but a way for left-handed bowlers to bowl slow wrist spin.
Fielders	Players who are placed around the field. The wicket-keeper and the bowler complete the fielding side of eleven players.

Players and Personnel

Runner	If a batsman has an injury that prevents him from running but not from batting, a runner is appointed from the batting team. According to the laws the runner must be a member of the nominated team who has (if possible) already batted. He must also wear the same external equipment (pads and helmet) as the injured batsman and he must carry a bat. Runners are no longer allowed in international matches. Injured players just retire hurt and can return to the batting side at the end of the innings if they feel well enough to bat.
Scorer	Essential member of the team for all cricket matches (sometimes a family member like you, sometimes a child or teacher from the same school, frequently the twelfth man). Responsible for keeping score to ensure the result is officially recorded. Scorers must concentrate hard throughout the match to ensure all the umpires' decisions are noted, including byes, no-balls, wides, boundaries and out decisions.
Twelfth man	The extra player who can replace an injured member of the fielding team. Traditionally, in order to avoid accusations of cheating, the twelfth man is not allowed to bowl, keep wicket or captain the side and he cannot be used as a simple substitute (as is done in football).

Players and Personnel

Umpires	Two independent people, usually one member of staff from each school at that level, who traditionally wear white coats but these days can just wear distinctive colours to distinguish them from the players on the pitch.
	They make decisions on wickets, runs, penalties, byes, no-balls, wides and any other issues (such as when to take a break or allow a player back into the game after a substitution) that may be needed throughout the match.
	It is very rare for umpires to disagree on any decision made; in general they take decisions based on a consensus view. At county and club level umpires are generally retired players but at international level they are often fit young men who devote their careers to this highly concentrated activity.

Players and Personnel

Wicket-keeper	The backstop of cricket. It is his responsibility to catch the ball after it has been bowled, assuming the batsman fails to make contact in a meaningful way and the bowler misses the stumps. In addition he is frequently in the best position to take catches and he can also help dismiss batsmen from the wicket by stumping or running them out.
XI	Latin numerals for eleven. As in 1st XI, 2nd XI, 3rd XI, Under 16 XI, etc. Used as part of the name for a specific team in a school or club.

Play

Balls	Cricket balls are made of stitched leather covering a hard interior with two linen seams that stand out from the leather. The seams allow the ball to bounce irregularly and help with both spinning the ball and swing bowling.
	Each innings is divided into overs made up of six balls per over (that is, the bowler will bowl the ball six times from one end of the pitch before the ball is transferred to a different bowler at the other end of the pitch). See also *no-balls* and *overs*.
Bat-pad	Describes a fielder who is in a position close to the batsman (usually at short leg) to catch the ball if it hits the bat, then the pad and rises to a catchable height.
	Also used as a defence against being given out lbw, by suggesting that the ball may have hit the bat first.
Beamer	A fast, full-toss ball which is aimed straight at the head of the batsman without bouncing on the pitch first. It is illegal and a no-ball will be called.
Block hole	Bowling the ball behind the batsman's feet, right at the stumps, is bowling into the block hole. This is where a yorker should land.

Play	
Bouncer	A fast, short-pitched ball that rises up, arriving close to the batsman's head. Such balls are limited to two per over.
Boundaries	Both the marked edges of the cricket ground and a term for scoring four runs by getting the ball past the boundary.
Bump ball	A ball which bounces up from the ground immediately after the batsman makes contact. The crowd may think a catch has been taken off a bump ball, but it is not given by the umpire, who, standing closer to the action, sees the ball bounce off the ground before being caught.
Bowling	The action of casting the ball forwards, with the arm held straight after wheeling it round the shoulder once. A cricketer is never allowed to throw the ball using a bent arm that then straightens, and must always bowl the ball correctly. Also known as a delivery.
Byes	Runs scored without the batsman making contact with the ball with his bat, hands or gloves. Leg byes are scored when the ball bounces off the batsman's body (anywhere except his gloves). Byes are scored when the batsmen are able to run even if the ball hasn't touched the bat or them. Sometimes four byes are scored when a fast bowler misses his target and the wicket-keeper and other fielders fail to stop the ball before it reaches the boundary.
Clean bowled	The description for a bowler breaking the stumps and dislodging the bails without the ball touching the batsman or his bat.
Dead balls	After an incident, the ball will be declared dead to stop the bowling team re-starting until the contentious matter has been resolved.

Play

Declaring/ declaration	Any team which believes it has scored enough runs to enable it to beat the opposition has the option of declaring or stopping batting. Team A can then make the other team bat and if they succeed in getting Team B out twice before they have overtaken Team A's score, Team A will win the match without needing their second innings. This is used in matches lasting more than 3 days, when a team gains a big lead; this option is not available or even sensible in limited-over matches.
Extras	Wides and no-balls give extra runs to the batting team over and above those actually run by the two batsmen. Byes and leg byes (see earlier in this section) are also recorded as extras. For wides and no-balls, the umpire will indicate when either offence occurs, and in both cases a single run is added to the score and an extra ball has to be bowled by the offending bowler. In addition, penalties can be awarded to give extra runs in limited-over cricket; two runs are awarded in domestic 40 over matches and in Twenty20 cricket the no-ball is followed by a free hit, meaning the batsman cannot be out, just as if it was another no-ball being bowled.
Feather	A very light touch of the bat on the ball, a snick is a similar light touch but the batsman is more likely to feel it and the fielders to hear it.
Follow on	In games lasting more than three days with two innings per team, a team scoring high runs can force the opposition to follow on and bat again if they don't get within 200 runs of their first innings score.
Full toss	A delivery that reaches the batsman without having hit the pitch first. Most difficult to handle when bowled by a fast bowler of course.
Half volley	A fuller-length delivery that is likely to be played off the front foot with an attacking shot from the batsman.

Play

Innings	Each match is divided into innings (one or two for each team depending on the length of the match). Innings are divided into an assigned number of *overs*. For limited-over cricket, between 20 and 50. See » https://en.wikipedia.org/wiki/Limited_overs_cricket for full details of all the variations around the world. There is only a single innings for each team in limited-over versions of the game. At Test matches, overs are unlimited, but at least 90 have to be bowled during a normal day's play for the team to keep within the regulations. If they fail to bowl sufficient overs in a day's play, the team can be punished, even fined, and the lost overs can be added to the number of overs required to be bowled on the following day.
Leg byes	Additional runs scored when the ball bounces off the batsman's body (anywhere except his bat, hands or gloves) and then the batsmen run between the stumps scoring a run each time they complete a traverse of the pitch, or the ball crosses the boundary to score four.
Limited overs	See the information above under *innings*.
Lower order	The batsman at the end of the batting order, usually bowlers lacking good batting skills.
Match	A game of cricket between two teams; it can last for an afternoon – the standard match at school level – or anything up to five days for a full Test match.
Middle order	Batsmen numbered 4–7 on the batting order list.

Play

No-balls   The umpires will call no-ball if the heel of the bowler's front foot lands on or in front of the popping crease (the front line of the batting crease).

However, the front foot can be raised over the line as long as the heel does not go beyond the popping crease.

He will also call no-ball for any of the following actions, if:

- the bowler's back foot is touching or outside the return crease;

- a full toss is bowled – a ball which does not bounce – from a fast bowler reaching the batsman at waist height or above. However, a waist-high full toss is permissible from a slower bowler, as long as it does not go above the batsman's shoulder. If it does, then the umpire will call a no-ball.

- the bowler does not notify the umpire of a change in their mode of delivery. For example, if a player says they are a right-arm bowler to the umpire and then bowls with their left arm, the umpire can call a no-ball.

- the umpire believes the bowler is throwing the ball.

- the bowler throws the ball to the striker's end before entering their delivery stride.

- the ball bounces more than twice before it reaches the batsman, or rolls along the ground towards him.

- the ball stops in front of the batsman without having touched the bat.

- the wicket-keeper encroaches beyond the stumps before the ball has been struck by the batsman or has passed the stumps.

- more than two fielders are positioned on the leg side behind square,

  and finally, if

- the umpire deems the bowler to be bowling dangerously and unfairly.

Play

No-balls	An *extra* run is given to the batting side and the bowler has to bowl an additional ball. The umpire will call out 'no-ball' and indicate it by holding one arm outstretched. In One day Internationals and Twenty20 limited-overs cricket, in the immediate next ball, the batsman can only get out as if the ball was another no-ball, i.e. he could be run out, or out handled the ball, hit the ball twice or obstructing the field. The freedom this gives allows the batsman to hit out without fear, which makes for exciting shots. This follow up ball is called a *free hit* and this rule came into international limited-over cricket in October 2007.
Overs	The period of a match defined as six legally bowled balls, after which the umpire will call out 'Over' (hence the name) and the fielders will move and the next bowler will deliver balls from the opposite end of the pitch to the second batsman. The time taken for each over to be completed will vary in length depending on the speed of the bowler. Curiously, slow bowlers actually bowl their overs faster than fast bowlers because their run-up is so much shorter. Some matches are defined as limited-overs matches, where the maximum number of overs bowled is set between 20 and 50 overs for each team.
Out of his ground	A batsman standing out of his ground is standing outside the popping crease and can be dismissed by the bails being removed from the wicket behind him either by the ball being thrown at the stumps, or by a fielder dislodging the bails with the ball in his hand.
Penalties	With the changes to the laws in 2000, penalties were introduced over and above the extras for wides and no-balls. These penalties are used to discourage what is known as gamesmanship, the attempt to gain an unfair advantage by such means as time wasting, pitch damage, ball tampering, etc. You'll find a full list of these in the Sue Porter's Guide to Scoring document available on download from our website.

Play

Run(s)	Every time the batsmen cross over and reach their respective creases at the opposite ends of the pitch, a run is scored. Every time the ball crosses over the boundary more runs are scored, four if the ball has hit the ground en route to the boundary or six if it goes over the boundary whilst remaining airborne. The umpire will indicate how many runs are scored if the ball goes over the boundary (see umpire signals later in the book).
Run out	If the fielding team break the wicket with the ball dislodging one or both of the bails when the batsman is outside the crease (either by stepping outside to bat or in the middle of running between the wickets), he is deemed run out.
	Either the wicket-keeper or another fielder can throw down the wicket from a distance for a more spectacular dismissal. The ball can also be thrown to the bowler's end of the pitch where the bowler or another fielder can run a batsman out if he is shy of the crease or out of his ground (i.e. still running between the wickets).
Run-up	Every bowler takes several paces before he bowls. The ground he covers during this is known as his run-up. Before a match, fast bowlers in particular will be seen pacing out from the wicket and leaving small markers on the ground; these mark the start of their run-up and will be moved back if they start to bowl no-balls by overstepping the crease.
Side	Another name for a team of cricketers. There are two sides in a cricket match.
Spin	Slow bowlers spin the ball using their fingers or wrists to make the ball change direction after it hits the pitch. Off-spin and leg-spin are varieties of spin bowling. See the bowling guide starting on page 87 for more information.
Super over	An additional over bowled at the end of a limited-over match to bring about a result if scores are tied. See our full description on page 55. Super overs are not generally used in school matches.

Play

Taking guard	The batsman on strike takes guard in front of his wicket as he awaits the ball being bowled at him. With guidance from the umpire standing at the bowler's end of the pitch, he may mark the pitch using the toe of his bat or his shoes, to ensure he keeps his feet and bat in the correct positions to protect the wicket.
Tea/lunch/ drinks breaks	A break in play is made to allow the two teams and the umpires to take refreshments, something to eat and drink. Cricket teas are legendary (more on this later). In addition, during long matches and in hot weather, drinks breaks are taken during the match, but in this case the players remain on the pitch for this short interval.
	At Test matches the crowd frequently treats this short time as an opportunity for a comfort break and a chance to purchase their next beverage.

Three departments	The three departments of cricket are batting, bowling and fielding. Used when describing how a team has played. A top team plays well in all three departments!
Top order	The top three batsmen on the batting order.

Play

The toss (and match timings)	The toss is the toss of a coin for the captains to choose whether to bat or bowl. For the purpose of interpreting the laws, *before the toss* is any time before the toss on the day the match is expected to start or, in the case of a one-day match, on the day the match is due to take place. *Before the match* is any time before the toss, not restricted to the day on which the toss is to take place. *During the match* is at any time after the toss until the conclusion of the match, whether play is in progress or not. They're a picky lot, these cricketers!
Wicket	The wicket is the combination of the stumps and bails as described previously. However the term *taking a wicket* is used to describe the dismissal of the batsman from the field. A batsman is said to lose his wicket, or be out. He is then replaced by another member of the team until all eleven have batted and ten have lost their wickets, which marks the end of that team's innings.
	Commentators frequently debate the use of the term *wicket* to describe the pitch; regardless of the inaccuracy, they still do it regularly. For instance, they talk about the batsman coming down the wicket to meet a ball delivery.
Wides	The ball is said to have gone wide when the ball is bowled so wide of the striker that he is unable to play a normal cricket shot. An extra run will be awarded to the batting side if this occurs and the bowler will have to bowl an additional ball. The position of the return crease is a good guideline for the width of the ball in relation to the wicket.
	In some competitions, the laws of cricket are modified so that any ball delivered over the batsman's head height is a wide ball but a second fast ball above shoulder height in an over is a no-ball (e.g. in international Twenty20 cricket and IPLT20). In international one-day cricket and in Test cricket, two fast-pitched short balls per over are allowed before no-ball is called, and again any ball over head height is a wide.

Some other cricketing terms

Cricket is such an ancient game that all sorts of quirky descriptions have become commonplace and so here are few of the terms used by commentators on TV and radio; hopefully I will demystify some of these for you:

Bowling a maiden over. Nothing to do with chatting up girls, this refers to an over in which the bowler succeeds in bowling all six balls without the batsman scoring any runs. There are also *maiden* terms for the first innings a batsman plays for his team (a maiden innings) and the first time he scores 100 (a maiden century).

Caught and bowled. If a batsman hits the ball in such a way that the bowler can catch it before it touches the ground he is adjudged out caught and bowled.

Caught in the slips. Nothing to do with lacy underwear, if a batsman is caught by one of the players standing in the slip cordon or slips (see the fielding diagram on page 101), he is said to be caught in the slips.

Century. One hundred runs scored by a single batsman.

Century stand. One hundred runs scored by two players together, a combination of their personal scores and extras.

Close of play. This is the term used to describe the timing of the end of a day's play. Stumps are pulled at close of play (i.e. when the end of the time allotted for playing is reached; 6.30 or 7 pm for Test matches in Britain and 6.30 pm for most other games).

A dot ball. See the scoring instructions for details, but if the commentator mentions a dot ball, he means the batsman hasn't hit and scored runs off a legally delivered ball. This will be recorded by the scorer putting a dot on the score sheet. Six dot balls make a maiden over.

Double century. Two hundred runs scored by one batsman.

Drawing stumps. Nothing to do with this book's wonderful illustrator, but the term applied to pulling the stumps out of the pitch at the close of play.

Fall of wicket. When a batsman is out, his wicket is said to fall (logical if you think about the bails falling off the stumps), and in commentary you will hear the term *fall of wicket* refer to its timing in the match, either in relation to the number of overs that have been bowled at that point, the number of runs scored or the actual time of day.

First-class games. Top-flight county and Test teams are described as first-class teams. This is a very specific description, as some smaller or minor county teams are not counted within this group. It dates from an MCC meeting in 1894 which designated the current leading teams at that time as first class.

According to the ICC, the following matches of three or more days' duration shall be regarded as first class, subject to the provisions of the first-class match definition being complied with. The list below is not exhaustive and covers tournaments rather than one-off fixtures. It is therefore merely indicative of the matches which would fall into the first-class definition.

i)   Test matches

ii) ICC Intercontinental Cup matches

iii) Matches by 'A' teams of Full Member countries against teams adjudged First-Class (including the 'A' team of another Full Member country)

iv) In all Full Member Countries Matches against teams adjudged First-Class played by official touring teams

v)   In Australia Pura Cup matches between states

vi) In Bangladesh National Cricket League matches between divisions

vii) In England and Wales County Championship matches between counties MCC v any First-Class county Oxford University v Cambridge University Cambridge, Durham, Loughborough and Oxford University Centres of Cricketing Excellence v any First-Class county

viii) In India Ranji Trophy matches between states Duleep Trophy matches between zones Irani Trophy match (winner of previous Ranji Trophy against Rest of India)

ix) In New Zealand State Championship matches between provinces

x) In Pakistan Quaid-e-Azam Trophy (Grade I) matches between regions Patron's Trophy (Grade I) matches between departments Pentangular Cup matches between leading teams from the other first-class tournaments

xi) In South Africa SuperSport Series matches between franchises CSA Provincial Cup matches between provinces

xii) In Sri Lanka Premier League Division I matches between clubs Inter Provincial Tournament matches between provinces

xiii) In West Indies Carib Beer Cup/International Series matches between countries

xiv) In Zimbabwe Logan Cup between areas

There are currently 18 first-class counties in the UK, see the link that follows for more information.

>> https://atheart.lv.com/sport/lv-county-championship-fixtures-2015

Getting your eye in. This refers to a batsman getting used to seeing the bowler bowling at him and seeing the trajectory and speed of the ball well (nothing to do with false eyes, although batsmen frequently replace contact lenses on the pitch these days and look as if they are replacing eyeballs!).

Getting off the mark. Refers to a batsman scoring his first run(s) in an innings.

Half century. Fifty runs scored by one player.

Hat trick. If a bowler succeeds in taking three wickets with three successive balls bowled, he is said to have taken a hat trick of wickets. After two wicket balls he is said to be on a hat trick.

In the slot. Bowlers aiming the ball straight at the stumps close to the wicket are bowling in the slot. Bowling here gives them an excellent chance of taking a wicket.

Leg cutter. A fast ball which bounces back towards the batsman's legs.

Long hop. Another description for a slow bouncing ball.

Off cutter. A fast ball which bounces away from the batsman towards the offside of the pitch.

Out for a duck. The batsman gets out without scoring any runs. An ancient description based on the shape of a duck's egg being a similar shape to the number 0, the term has applied to cricket from its earliest days. An innovation in Kerry Packer's Australian televised cricket series in the late 1970s resulted in many TV companies around the world using the picture of a sad duck waddling off the screen to accompany the batsman who is out for a duck, on his return to the pavilion. Nowadays county cricket grounds with electronic scoreboards replace them with a similar picture when this occurs.

Out for a golden duck. The batsman gets out to the first ball he faces without scoring any runs. Diamond, silver, gold, bronze and platinum ducks are also terms used for varying types of zero score. These seem to vary around the world and there are also royal ducks and laughing ducks!

Night watchman. No, not the security team at the ground; this is a batsman from lower down the batting order who is sent in to bat when a batsman is out near the end of a day's play during a county or test match.

A pair. Getting out for a duck in both innings of a match.

Scores. Listening to cricket commentaries on radio or watching a match on television, you will hear the score described in very specific ways. In the UK, the batting side will have their score described using the number of runs they have scored first, followed by the number of wickets lost. So if a team has scored one hundred runs, but lost three wickets, the commentator would say 'They are one hundred for three'. However in Australia they would reverse this and say 'three for one hundred' just to confuse us. Scoring descriptions do vary around the globe.

In the UK the fielding side would view this score as three for one hundred and the bowler's statistics are always described using the number of wickets taken first. If a bowler has taken all three of the wickets and only had twenty-five runs scored against him, his figures will be described by the commentators as 'three for twenty-five'.

Because a match can be won either by scoring more runs or by losing fewer wickets on the same score, the descriptions of results vary and a team can be said to have won the match by thirteen runs, or have beaten the opposition by three wickets. The description usually depends on who bats first. For instance:

X county scores 236 runs for 8 wickets
Y county scores 239 runs for 6 wickets
The result is Y beat X by 4 wickets (in other words they still had 4 wickets in hand after passing the other team's score).

X county scores 237 for 5 wickets
Y county scores 232 all out
X county wins by 5 runs

In limited-over cricket only, the following outcome is possible but very unusual:

X county scores 236 runs for 8 wickets
Y county scores 236 runs for 9 wickets
X county beats Y by 1 wicket

A sitter. Actually nothing to do with sitting around, as this is the description for an easy catch. It just means the fielder doesn't need to move an inch in order to catch the ball.

Shy of the crease. Nothing to do with bashful cricketers, this is a phrase used to describe a batsman who is running between the wickets to score runs, but fails to get back behind the crease in time to prevent himself being run out.

Stand. As in a *fine stand,* a *century stand,* etc. When two players stay together at the wicket during an innings and score a good number of runs between them, their stay at the wicket is called a stand. Usually innings only becomes stands after runs in double figures have been scored. A stand is also, of course, an area of seating for spectators in professional cricket grounds and these can become muddled if you are listening to commentary on the radio: 'Sussex have a fine stand' could mean that two Sussex players have played well together or that the spectators are housed in high quality surroundings. There's a fine line between a century stand and a centenary stand!

Tail. No, we're not talking animals playing cricket, this is merely the term used to describe the last four batsmen on the batting list or order. Usually they are bowlers whose batting skills can be less well developed than those of their teammates; occasionally though the tail will wag and those lower down the batting order will hit lots of runs to surprise and delight everyone in their team. The fielding team is less impressed by a wagging tail of course!

Wickets in hand. This describes the number of batsmen left in the batting team who have yet to bat; if a team has four players out, they have six wickets in hand.

Yorker. Not a resident of York City but a bowling delivery that travels far down the pitch – otherwise known as a full delivery – and lands near the toes of the batsman.

Preparing a field for cricket

Cricketing history advises us that in order to prepare a field for playing cricket, the following actions need to be taken:

1. The field is mown.

2. A square in the middle of the field is mown even shorter.

3. A 22-yard pitch on the square is mown shortest of all and gives the appearance of having had all the grass (almost) completely eliminated from its surface.

In common parlance the pitch is frequently referred to as the wicket, but this is really incorrect, even though you may hear it said by both professional commentators and crowd members alike. The wicket should just refer to the stumps and bails together. However, commentators will discuss the quality of the wicket, how well a ball will bounce on it and the likelihood of it being good for the spin bowlers, for instance.

Professional cricket grounds are never square and are frequently inside oval-shaped stadiums, so the term *square* is rarely an accurate description and the term *oblong* or *rectangle* would be much more appropriate. All grounds are marked with an oblong of shorter grass that is marked out as the square. Once the mowing has taken place the pitch is marked with white lines (see the pitch illustration on the next page). On major grounds, several pitches will be marked out inside the square; these allow for one to be preserved for important matches while others are used for practice. Not every pitch is in the centre of the ground or the centre of the square which means some fields have shortened boundaries on one side of the pitch that batsman are keen to exploit whenever they get the chance.

Preparation of the pitch continues with two white parallel lines or creases being marked at each end of the pitch. These indicate the areas from which a bowler may safely bowl. His delivery stride must have some part of his front foot, whether grounded or raised, behind the front or popping crease and his back foot must land within and not touching the side or return crease or he will be deemed to have delivered a no-ball. The front or popping crease marks the area behind which a batsman may safely stand (see the details on being stumped and run out on page 82).

The boundary of the field is usually marked either by another painted white line, or by a rope or fence. Traditional English village cricket grounds are sometimes bounded by a white picket fence. The size of the field on which the game is played varies from ground to ground but the pitch is always a rectangular area of 22 yards (20.12 m) in length and 10 ft (3.05 m) in width.

The popping crease is marked 1.22 m in front of the stumps at either end, with the stumps set along the bowling crease. The return creases are marked at right angles to the popping and bowling creases and are measured 1.32 m either side of the middle stumps.

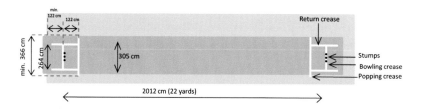

Two sets of three wooden sticks (usually made from ash) called *stumps* are inserted at either end of the pitch and the umpires place two bridging pieces of moulded wood, called *bails*, on both sets of stumps at the beginning of the match. These form the wickets. They stand 71.1 cm high and the three stumps measure 22.86 cm wide in total.

The laws of cricket bar watering the pitch during a match. As the pitch dries out initially, batting becomes easier as any moisture disappears. However, over the course of a four- or five-day match, the pitch begins to crack, then crumble and become dusty. This type of pitch is colloquially known as a dust bowl or minefield. It greatly favours the bowlers of course, particularly spin bowlers who can obtain large amounts of traction on the surface and make the ball spin obliquely a very long way.

The use of a light or heavy roller can also change the nature of the pitch. Traditionally four men would pull the heavy roller over the pitch to smooth down any bumps before a game commenced. These days professional clubs have mechanised rollers that the groundskeeper drives over the pitch, much like the sit-on lawn mowing machines that are also used to maintain the grounds. No roller is allowed back on the pitch until each innings is complete, and some captains may choose not to use the roller again if they can see the pitch is beginning to break up as described above, which will give their bowlers a better chance of dismissing the opposition.

County and Test grounds also have the benefit of special machines to remove water from the pitch after a rain storm. These machines push the water with squeegee foam rollers and scoop it up into collecting tanks, greatly speeding up the time it takes to restart a game after a rain interruption. At schools and smaller clubs, the ground staff may simply use a heavy rope dragged across the ground to move water from the pitch prior to a restart.

The changes in the relative difficulties of batting and bowling as the state of the pitch changes during a match are one of the primary strategic considerations that the captain of the team who wins the coin toss will take into account when deciding which team will bat first.

Once the toss has been taken and the decision on which team will bat is made, the game of cricket begins. Two batsmen from the batting team come out and stand at either end of the pitch behind their respective creases, and the fielding team spread themselves around the ground.

See the diagram below showing the various areas of the pitch and some fielding zones such as the infield area and the close infield area. The outer oval is the outfield section of a cricket ground. Batsman can be right handed (R) or left handed (L).

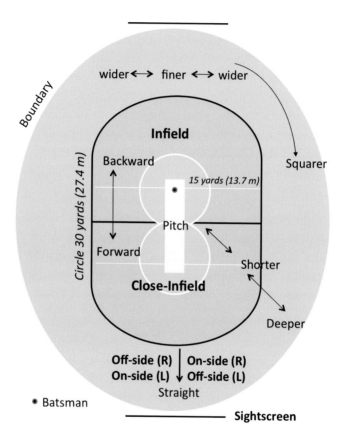

The aims of the game

The main aims of cricket are scoring runs and taking wickets. In limited-over cricket, the team or side that scores the most runs in a match, or loses the least wickets while scoring the same number of runs will win. The only exception is during matches that are disrupted by bad weather, when a truly amazing calculation system is invoked to bring about a result. The system was invented by Messrs Duckworth and Lewis and I explain more about this on page 145.

At any given time there are two batsmen on the field of play: one striking and one non-striking. It is their job to protect the wicket with their bats. In order to score runs the batsman on strike, that is facing the bowler, has to hit the ball away with his bat and then run the length of the pitch, crossing over with his fellow batsman en route. Each time the batsmen cross over and reach or touch their bat down on the ground inside the safe area behind the popping crease at the opposite end, a run is scored. If they fail to touch the ground with their bat whilst still standing outside the zone, they can be run out, so this is an essential move for every running batsman to complete.

If the ball crosses the boundary line or rope, either running at ground level or having bounced on the pitch at least once first, four runs are scored. In this case, the batsmen do not have to run and cross over for the runs to count on the score sheet. If the ball crosses the boundary without touching the ground after leaving the batsman's bat, it will score six runs. With this additional scoring ability it is possible to score 36 runs in one over, but this has rarely been achieved and certainly never at junior level to my knowledge.

Runs can also be scored when the ball has not been hit by the bat. If the fielders do not retrieve the ball immediately and the batsmen manage to run the length of the pitch, they can add to the runs scored. If the ball has glanced off any part of the batsman other than his bat or glove these runs are called leg byes, even if the ball hits the batsman's head! If the ball has not touched the batsman at all, he can still run and these runs are described as byes.

It is not unusual in schools cricket for a fast bowler to defeat not only the batsman but also his own team's wicket-keeper and for four byes to be awarded to the batting team as the ball speeds towards and over the boundary without anyone touching it. Whilst this demonstrates the speed of the fast bowler it does nothing for his credibility as a team player and he will often be ticked off by his teammates and coach for bowling too fast or not straight enough and for being out of control in general!

In addition, if the fielders throwing the ball back to the wickets aim badly and other fielders are unable to stop the ball, overthrows can occur and the batsmen can continue to run until the ball is returned correctly to the wicket area. At junior level, it's not unusual for the ball to fly over the wicket more than once without being stopped and lots of additional runs get scored as a result, until throwing and catching skills are developed.

Balls that cross the boundary can also get lost in surrounding undergrowth in rural country grounds, and local rules may allow the batsmen to continue running until the ball is retrieved. However, if the ball is obviously lost, the umpires may intervene and declare the ball dead until it can be found or replaced with a ball of similar age. Once the ball is declared dead, the batsmen cannot score more runs by continuing to traverse the pitch.

There are two other ways in which runs can be scored by the batting side:

No-balls generally occur if the bowler oversteps the popping crease in his delivery stride with his front foot, or his back foot lands outside or touching the return crease (see the glossary for more information). The umpire is supposed to shout 'No-ball' clearly and hold his arm out sideways so that the batsman knows he may take a mighty swing at the ball, since when 'No-ball' has been called, neither batsman can be out unless they: handle the ball (law 33); hit the ball twice (law 34); obstruct the field (law 37) or are run out (law 38). All of these transgressions will result in a summary dismissal by the umpires. In the 2013 review of the laws a new no-ball offence was brought in to cover the eventuality of the bowler hitting the non-facing batsman's wicket during a delivery stride (i.e. he gets too close to the wicket and knocks the bails off as he charges past to bowl).

No-balls in Twenty20 matches will result in the batsman being given a free hit at the next ball bowled. This means he cannot be caught or stumped out, although he could still be run out, and this allows batsmen to hit out freely at these balls. New spectators can be surprised when a batsman appears to have been caught out but remains at the crease. If you're watching one of these matches, this will probably be the explanation for such an incident.

Bowling a wide

Wides are balls bowled so wide of the wicket that a batsman couldn't reasonably be expected to hit them, even if he wanted to. The creases are a guideline to this, but as batsman frequently move outside their crease to play the ball, they can often bring what looks like a wide ball to the inexperienced spectator into play. Balls which arrive over shoulder height can also be deemed wide or no-balls (see the glossary for more details).

Both of these faulty bowling deliveries result in one run being allotted to the batting team as an extra run added to the team's total score; if the batsman uses his bat and running energy he can score more runs and these are added to his personal score and the team total.

As the bowler has to bowl an additional delivery for each wide or no-ball before an over is complete, it is not unheard of for 10 or 12 balls to be bowled in an over at junior level (which naturally makes the novice scorer's job even more difficult).

At the end of the batting team's innings, the total number of runs scored by all these methods is added up. When matches are scheduled to be played over more than a day, each side gets two innings to bat and the runs scored in both innings are added together to make the total the second team has to beat during its two innings. Captains who are convinced their side has scored sufficient runs to allow them to dismiss the opposition without being beaten can declare.

The declaration is made and the batting team swop places with their opposition. If the first batting team score sufficient runs and get the other team out before they score within 200 runs of the first team's total, then the latter can enforce a follow on and make the second team bat again. If they get them all out again before they reach the original team's first innings total, then the first batting team beats the second by an innings and the number of runs that match the differential between their scores.

In one-day games, where each side bats just once, the second team has to get at least one run more than the opposition, before losing ten wickets, in order to win the match.

If both teams score the same number of runs and the team batting second has lost all its wickets, the match is a tie and (in limited-overs only) the side losing fewer wickets is the winner. If both sides score the same number of runs and lose the same number of wickets, super overs can be bowled to bring a limited-over game to an absolute conclusion. In this case, each team nominates three batsmen and a bowler for the super overs. Obviously the whole team is allowed to field.

The two teams then return to the crease. For one over (six balls), the first team's nominated bowler delivers his six balls, while the second team's nominated batsmen protect the wickets. Then the second team fields and bowls an over while the first team bats. The team that scores the most runs is awarded the match. Wickets can be taken as normal but a team's super over ends if it loses two wickets, and that team will lose the match if their score is lower than their opposition's total when the second wicket falls.

Instead of equally dividing the points between the two participating teams, the winning team of the super overs takes all the points, but the result is still counted as a tie in the record books. The super over was first used in 2008 in Twenty20 cricket as the method for breaking a tie. In other formats of cricket, if the set number of overs has been played or play is terminally stopped by weather or bad light, that game is tied. This is a very rare occurrence and has been recorded just twice in Test cricket.

In unlimited-over or timed matches there is another possibility, a draw; for schools cricket, however, this will only apply if the match is not a limited-over match. In such matches the result can be a draw if the side batting second does not pass the total of the other side but has not lost all its wickets at the close of play. In this instance, a team that knows it is unable to win can save a draw by managing to have two or more players not out at the end of the innings. The match is then drawn regardless of the total of runs accumulated by both sides.

The stumps (which form a key part of the game) have specific names that will be referred to in radio or TV commentary. A right-handed batsman usually stands to face a right-handed bowler with his body placed in such a position that either his body or bat is in front of the leg stump. The cricket ground (see page 23) is divided into an on or leg side and an off side. The on side is the side the batsman will naturally hit towards (i.e. for a right-handed batsman to his left and rear as he faces the bowler with his left shoulder) and the off side is therefore out in front of the batsman, to his right as he hits the ball down the pitch. Fielders are given names associated with their positions on the field, so mid-off and mid-on exist alongside long-off, short-leg, etc. The on or leg and off locations are shown with reference to a right-handed batsman on the diagram on page 101.

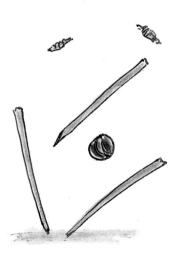

Types of cricket

There are numerous variations of the sport played throughout the world that include indoor cricket, French cricket, beach cricket, Kwik cricket and all sorts of card, dice and board games that have been inspired by game of cricket. In some of these variants, the rules are changed to make the game playable with limited resources or to render it more convenient and enjoyable for the participants.

Indoor cricket is an eight-a-side game played in special courts enclosed by tight string netting in a sports arena. It can be quite formal and has set rules but many of the outdoor variants of cricket are very informal:

Families and teenagers play backyard cricket in suburban gardens (which they call yards in North America) or on driveways, and the cities of India and Pakistan play host to countless games of gully cricket or tape ball in their long narrow streets. Sometimes the rules are improvised; for example, it may be agreed that fielders can catch the ball with one hand after one bounce and still claim a wicket; or if only a few people are available then everyone may field while the players take it in turns to bat and bowl. Tennis balls and homemade bats are often used, and a variety of objects may serve as wickets. For example, the batter's legs are used as wickets in French cricket, which did not in fact originate in France. It is a game usually played by small children.

In Kwik cricket, the bowler does not have to wait for the batsman to be ready before a delivery, leading to a faster, more exhausting game designed to appeal to children. It is often used in PE lessons at British schools. Another modification to increase the pace of the game is the tip and run, tipity run, tipsy run or tippy-go rule, in which the batter must run when the ball touches the bat, even if the contact is unintentional or slight. This rule, seen only in impromptu games, speeds the match up by removing the batsman's right to block the ball.

In Samoa a form of cricket called Kilikiti is played in which hockey stick-shaped bats are used, as they were in the original English cricket game. In Estonia, teams gather over the winter for the annual ice cricket tournament. The game juxtaposes the normal summer pursuit with harsh, wintry conditions. Rules are otherwise similar to those for the six-a-side game.

In addition, there is also tape ball and tennis ball cricket. Both variations use a tennis ball instead of a regular cricket ball to play. In tape ball cricket, the ball is additionally covered with electric insulating tape to make it more like a proper cricket ball. This variation was pioneered in Pakistan and is believed to have contributed greatly to Pakistan's famous production of fast bowlers, as children are brought up playing the game using a tape ball in which these skills are developed. The increasing popularity of the tape ball in informal, local cricket has transformed the way games are played in cricket-loving nations such as Pakistan, Bangladesh and India.

Last man stands is an exciting and easily accessible format of cricket designed for busy people. It's a Twenty20-style social game that only lasts just over 2 hours per match. You can find more about it in the web links at the end of the book.

Girls' and women's cricket

This is the fastest developing area of the game. The Lady Taverners U13 and U15 indoor (schools) and outdoor (clubs) girls' cricket competitions have given over 110,000 girls the opportunity to enjoy competitive cricket, many for the first time. The Lady Taverners charity has sponsored the ECB-run national girls' indoor and outdoor cricket competitions since 2003. Of course, as I've already explained in the history section, cricket has been a summer sport for girls and women for many centuries, and has been taught at private schools in the UK for over a century, although it is far less common in state schools. Women's cricket clubs have been around for well over a century too, with the first, the White Heather Club, forming in Yorkshire in 1887.

The ECB has recently announced a new development; a new Women's Cricket Super League will start in 2016. During its first season, the Women's Cricket Super League will be comprised solely of Twenty20 cricket and it will sit alongside the Royal London Women's One-Day County Cup and NatWest Women's County Twenty20 competitions. From 2017 onwards the structure will develop to both Twenty20 and 50-over formats. It's certainly a very exciting time for women's cricket and I can't wait to see how the game develops in the coming years.

Easy cricket

Easy cricket is the latest initiative from the England Cricket Board and it includes the following options:

- Beat the catches
- Continuous cricket
- Cricket circuit
- Cricket rounders
- Danish rounders
- French cricket
- Keep your yard clean
- Pairs batting
- Pairs cricket
- Street 20
- Diamond cricket
- Cardio cricket
- Wicketz

Wicketz is the latest innovation from the Lord's Taverners, who commissioned research that identified the 20 most disadvantaged areas of the UK, based on indices of multiple deprivation, anti-social behaviour, pupil attainment and engagement in sport. They found that financial deprivation was a huge barrier to community sports participation as young people were often unable to afford membership, equipment and venue fees. Following a successful two-year pilot in London, Wicketz will be expanded to support young people in these targeted 20 areas beginning with Hartlepool and Luton in 2015, with further expansion planned for 2016.

You can find more details of all these variants on the ECB website.

Disability cricket

The ECB supports all disabled cricketers and has a detailed leaflet advising all clubs on their role in this. You can find the leaflet link in our web links at the back of this book.

Finally, you can learn more about all the options for playing cricket that are available in the UK from the ECB website:
>> http://www.ecb.co.uk/development/get-into-cricket/

In addition the ECB website now includes information on inclusivity in general, under their One Game heading. This includes disability cricket, women's and girls' cricket and other aspects of the game that make it more inclusive and more relevant in the modern world. Check it out and you will discover all about what the cricket authorities are currently doing to help people from different backgrounds get involved in the game.

Cricket matches

5-Day, 4-Day, One-Day and Twenty20

As you will discover in this book, cricket is played over several different time scales. The longest – 5-day – is used for international Test matches. England county games last four days. One-day matches can last anything from 20 to 50 overs. International one-day matches and county one-day matches are 50 overs for each team. The Twenty20 game (i.e. 20 overs for each team) is an exciting form of the game, often played in the evening so people can come along after work to watch. It has slightly different rules from the other forms of the game, as I explain below.

Twenty20 or 20/20 Cricket

Currently the most popular form of the game for spectators, bringing in large crowds to cricket grounds around the world, Twenty20 cricket is played over just 40 overs (20 for each team) and requires good bowling and fielding skills as well as batsmen who can hit hard and fast. There is a bowling limit of a maximum of four overs per bowler, but as there is no limit on the number of bowlers, several can be used and some may only bowl one or two overs. Batting teams have just 20 overs to score as many runs as possible or until 10 of their number are out. This exciting game makes very good watching and is an ideal introduction to the professional game.

Teams currently playing International Twenty20 are (in order of status in the results lists at the time of publication): South Africa, Sri Lanka, Pakistan, India, England, Australia, West Indies, New Zealand, Bangladesh, Zimbabwe, the Netherlands, Ireland, Afghanistan, Scotland, Kenya, Canada and Bermuda; these rankings are constantly changing of course.

The Twenty20 World Cup is organised by international cricket's governing body, the International Cricket Council (ICC). The tournament consists of 16 teams, comprising all ten ICC full members and six other ICC members chosen through the ICC World Twenty20 Qualifier series of matches. The event is generally held every two years, and all matches are accorded full Twenty20 International status. The qualifying rounds for the 2016 cup have now been played and the qualifying teams are going to be Ireland, Scotland, Afghanistan, Hong Kong, the Netherlands and Oman. The 2014 Champions are Sri Lanka.

In the women's version of the competition, Australia are the current champions, with England, New Zealand, India, West Indies, Sri Lanka, South Africa and Pakistan completing the list of those playing. The next competition will take place in 2017 with the final being played at Lord's.

So now you know a bit more about types of cricket, let me give you some detail on the traditional game your young son or daughter will be taught at their school or club.

Most schools play limited-overs games against other schools, generally 50-over matches. However schools that have a long history of playing each other at regular annual fixtures may have always played a full day on a Saturday and these will be unlimited overs matches.

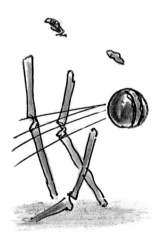

Equipment needed to play cricket

Development games including Kwik cricket and Wicketz allow children to learn something about the full game without the expense of purchasing a bespoke cricket kit. Children start out wearing t-shirts, shorts and trainers as they would for any other sporting activity. However, once they start to play proper cricket matches, or use the official hard ball, it will be preferable for them to have long trousers to protect their legs whilst wearing pads. Initially children learn to play using a tennis ball or other soft ball, but the use of the traditional cricket ball will require the wearing of protective equipment of all types.

Schools and clubs have a stock of kit for children to share initially, but keen cricketers will almost certainly insist on having all their own kit. This can all be quite expensive but will probably require the following basic kit purchases:

- A cricket bag. These are made of a similar construction to a nylon sports bag and have pockets for boots, clothing and an outside full length zippable pocket for the bat. Professional players have large trunks or suitcases for their kit that are nicknamed *coffins*. Junior players are unlikely to need these unless they are sufficiently talented to end up playing for county or country from an early age.
- 1 short-sleeved shirt or 1 long-sleeved shirt
- 1 long-sleeved sweater, preferably in school or club colours (this makes it more expensive naturally), or 1 sleeveless sweater
- 1 pair of cricket shoes. It's important they are properly constructed to protect the feet; ordinary trainers will not do this and broken toes may result.
- 1 pair of cricket trousers
- White socks
- 1 bat

- 1 set of leg pads
- 1 pair batting gloves
- 1 cap or hat
- 1 cricketer's protective box and pouch – for boys only.

This list should set up the keenest of players for their first season, but as the years go by additional specialised shoes, extra shirts, socks, trousers and so on will be needed to cope with practices, matches, and games lessons, all within a few days of each other.

As the chief sports supporter in your family, your role in all this is obvious. It will be up to you to restrain your child from buying equipment that is (a) too large, (b) too heavy and (c) too expensive!

Given total freedom of choice, a small boy will have little idea what size bat to buy, for instance, and may choose one that is too heavy for a long batting innings. Although he will grow rapidly and the weight of a bat will lessen proportionally, many boys return home from their first cricket match with aching arms, having swung the new bat around for longer than expected and having completely worn themselves out. You should be aware that boys will be drawn to the biggest and heaviest bat thinking it will improve their hit rate – sadly this is not the case and it will be down to you to persuade them to buy a smaller and lighter bat, even if it needs replacing after a few years as they grow. I'm sure girls are far more intelligent about these choices, but this advice applies just as much to them.

The desire to possess the most expensive bat in the rack, or the best-known brand of pads can be irresistible to the young player, just like the need for designer jeans and trainers. As a sensible parent you will resist such requests and only purchase reasonably priced kit (or even secondhand kit from the school or club secondhand shop) while they are growing. There is no guarantee your child will pursue a cricketing career past the first few years and the initial expenditure is impossible to recover in full, although the aforementioned secondhand shops will prove a good place to recycle unwanted kit in due course.

The most embarrassing part of the kit for boys is of course the box or groin protector. This protective moulded plastic or metal device is essential once boys are playing serious cricket but the advice of your friendly sports shop assistant will allay your son's fears when he is required to decide what size box he needs. Since he will probably not replace this item until he is old enough to go shopping alone, the initial purchase should allow for a certain amount of growth, but he will still need to be able to run whilst wearing it, so buying the correct size is important.

The addition of a jock strap or pouched underpants to hold the box in place may also be required, but this can be omitted if the embarrassment factor for your son is too great; a pair of tight-fitting underpants will do the job just as well. Just to make life simpler, specially designed protective underwear or shorts are now available that hold the box and two thigh pads (inner and outer).

As a cricketer's career develops and they become a regular member of the school or club side, their need for protective kit will increase. Not only will they need their own batting pads and gloves, they may also start to use forearm and thigh protection too. Although this doesn't compare with the kit required for American football, standard cricket kit does now include helmets.

Small children are unlikely to need helmets unless they have special features to protect (a fragile nose for instance), as very young fast bowlers are incapable of building up sufficient speed with the ball to cause too much damage, but the cricketing authorities do now recommend helmets for all young cricketers. Certainly once they get become teenagers, the fast bowlers' technique will have improved and they may get peppered around the head on a regular basis.

Headgear in general has certainly changed since the mid-20th century, with the addition of fielders' sun hats and helmets to the traditional cloth cap. Caps are still worn, but generally they are based on baseball hats these days, with the Australian baggy cloth cap being the other alternative. The broad-brimmed sun hats were introduced in Australia

to counteract sunstroke in the glaring heat of an antipodean summer and special cricketers' sunglasses also exist. The latter are anti-glare glasses with replaceable light-enhancing lenses for playing in low light conditions. They are not cheap, but can be readily replaced with some of the cheaper versions used by cyclists.

Shoes for cricket have changed significantly in recent years too and are no longer the heavy leather high-sided boots with steel toecaps that were worn in former times. The influence of running shoe technology is very apparent in modern cricket shoes, which now include 'lightweight ventilated uppers, superior cushioning, mid foot support and motion control technology' and shoes that claim to have been 'developed in conjunction with leading sports podiatrists'. The spikes are still removable from a spike plate embedded into the sole but can now be metal or plastic for different conditions. At one time there were bespoke boots for batting, bowling and fielding, but while bespoke bowling shoes remain, hybrid shoes for batsmen and fielders provide the main alternative.

Here's some advice on how to choose the best cricket shoes, I hope you find it useful. Various studies of footwear have come up with the following interesting results: people who run in old shoes are *less* likely to be injured than people who run in new ones; the more cushioning the shoes provides the *more* likely you are to injure yourself; and the thicker and harder the sole of your shoe, the worse your balance will become. Fast bowlers suffer from injuries as a result of their need to land hard as they bowl, but anecdotal evidence from basketball shows that ankle-protecting shoes actually weaken the ankles, so these would not be recommended for long-term wear.

It is therefore recommended that the cricketer's boots should be shoe cut for batting and fielding and high cut for bowling. However if your player does opt for the higher cut make sure they are doing some ankle strengthening exercises before taking to the pitch. Curiously it's recommended that barefoot practice for both bowling and fielding will actually be good for the feet and reduce foot injuries.

Cricketing spikes come in various lengths: a full spike; a half-spike (with spikes just at the front of the shoe); rubbers or pimples (no spikes as such, just rubber moulded grips) and finally, adjustable soles where you can remove metal spikes and replace them with rubber ones. It is recommended that fast bowlers use a full spike for extra stability when bowling. They should only consider other alternatives when playing on artificial surfaces. For other players the general rule is that the softer the surface, the more useful spikes will become and the harder the surface the less you'll need them.

Since too much cushioning has been proven to exacerbate injuries, you should avoid highly cushioned footwear with gel and air. A simple shoe with as thin a sole as possible is much less likely to injure a player.

Protection for the toes has gone out of fashion in recent years, but is definitely worth considering at more senior levels when fast bowlers could be hitting toes at over 90 mph. However it does increase the weight of the shoe and can make running a little more difficult.

Finally, players should never wear brand new shoes for an important match, but should always break them in slowly and use old shoes in this situation.

I appreciate this is an awful lot of detail to take in, but I hope you'll find it useful when helping your young player to select the right kit.

One final thought from us: the whole idea of wearing whites for cricket (actually more cream than pure white in colour) must have been invented by a man, since any self-respecting housewife would have immediately pointed out the total impracticality of choosing such a colour for playing a game in which players regularly throw themselves around on muddy and grassy fields. Indeed it's worth noting that the wearing of whites was not compulsory until the late 1800s. At least the cricket kit designers for the modern game seem to have realised this and the new kits for limited-over matches are far more colourful; both the England one-day teams (ladies and men) now play in blue. Purists are highly critical of these colourful kits and have termed this type of cricket pyjama cricket as a result!

I'll be giving you some information on grass stain removal and general care of kit later in the book, but you can go to page 114 if you want to read this now.

Playing a game

So now your young player has the kit and is ready to play, let's get into the details of playing a game. We've already given you an idea of earlier attempts at explaining the game to outsiders which have not always been very helpful. We'll try to use the terminology you hear during cricket commentary on radio and television, and hopefully we'll explain it in simple-to-understand detail.

There are two teams of 11 players allowed on the pitch. The laws allow for much larger team squads to be named but only 11 members of the fielding team are allowed on the pitch at any one time. There is also a nominated twelfth man in each team. As I explained earlier, if a player is injured or ill during a match, the twelfth man is allowed to replace him as a fielder. The twelfth man is not allowed to bowl, nor to act as wicket-keeper or captain but he can help keep the team complete by fielding. However, he cannot join the batting line-up. If an injured or ill player leaves the field with the umpires' permission he is allowed to be substituted, and to return to the field in due course.

At school matches the twelfth man is often a less able cricketer than the rest of the team, since if he was really talented he would either be a member of the team already, or be in another school team like the 2nd XI. He is sometimes brought along for his ability to keep score (cricket scorecards have a reputation for being quite complicated and suit a mathematical rather than a sporting brain). Players with the family support to bring along snacks and drinks for their teammates make very popular twelfth men.

The only time a chosen twelfth man is of equal skill to his team is when they are playing in a limited-over Cup or competition match. There are several competitions for young players run by the MCC and Lords' Taverners in England including the HMC Twenty20 Competition. When playing in these games it is essential that the reserve player is as skilled as his peers, since he may be needed to play if one of them gets injured or needs a comfort break. Even so the twelfth man rarely gets to play, but he can take pleasure in being part of a senior and hopefully successful team. The laws relating to substitutions are very detailed so I won't dwell on them in any great detail in this book, but they can be explored further at:

>> http://www.rulesofcricket.co.uk/the_rules_of_cricket/the_rules_of_cricket_law_2.htm

Any player who leaves the field (for whatever reason) must gain the umpires' permission to do so, and whatever time they spend off the field, they will not be allowed to bowl again until they have spent an equivalent amount of time back on the field.

Of course if a player leaves the field during normal play (i.e. going outside the boundary to collect a ball that has gone for four or six) he will not be deemed to have left the field without permission and will be allowed back onto the field of play without hindrance.

Cricket matches

Every cricket match needs a ball and the construction of cricket balls has changed over the years. Modern balls used in day/night games are now sometimes covered in white leather, and pink balls are also available. Indoor balls are made from PU plastic centres and are covered in yellow leather. Coaches can also now purchase two-coloured balls for spin and swing ball training; they have one smooth and one rough side and a distinct seam. Other training balls also exist. If you're keen to learn more, you can find full details on:

>> http://www.kookaburra.biz/en-gb/cricket/gear/men/kookaburra-cricket-balls/all-cricket-balls/

So, cricket is a team sport and the team that scores the most runs and gets the other team out wins the game. It's that simple. All cricket matches are divided into at least two sections or innings. However, these two sections are rarely equal in terms of actual time spent batting or fielding. The innings are sub-divided into overs, and if the overs are limited to a set number to be played in each innings this will be a limited-over match. Standard limits are 20 overs (the Twenty20 game), and 50 overs per innings (used currently for one-day international matches and English county one-day games since 2014). In Australia they have 45-over matches and there are similar variations around the world.

A standard day's play for a 4-day county match is from 11 am until 6 pm with a break for lunch between 1 pm and 1.40 pm and for tea from 3.40 to 4 pm. However some Twenty20 matches start later (sometimes as late as 5 pm) and continue well into the evening using floodlights. At schools level, games will generally start just after lunch (around 1.30 pm) and may continue until approximately 6.30 or 7 pm depending on the type of match being played. You need to be aware that you will be spending an entire afternoon at the match and much of your evening will be lost too, if you go along to support your youngster at a school game. Generally schools play 30-, 40- or 50-over cricket currently although the Twenty20 game is also becoming popular.

Before the game can commence, the two captains meet with the umpires to toss a coin to decide which team will bat first; this is known as the toss. The home team captain usually tosses the coin and the away team captain will call heads or tails. The winner can then choose whether to bat or field first. Sometimes if no one has a coin available they will spin a bat instead and call to predict which way the bat will land (i.e. splice up or down) but this is rare.

There are two umpires for all cricket games; for school matches it will usually be the games teacher who has accompanied the team to the match and the coach or teacher from the host school's team who perform this function. Some schools have teachers who don't coach cricket but do umpire. At clubs, team parents with knowledge of the laws can get asked to umpire.

If you are watching or listening to Test match commentary you will hear reference to the third umpire, or TV umpire. In addition there is a match referee who has responsibility for all matters of discipline, but it is the umpires who have the final veto over all decisions including whether a game can continue in bad weather. The third umpire remains in the pavilion with access to the television recording of the game and is able to review difficult decisions on wickets and high scoring hits for the umpires on the pitch. They review the footage in slow motion to assist with run-out decisions; they check suspected wickets to ensure the ball has been correctly bowled as laid down in the laws and can advise the on-pitch umpires whether a leg-before-wicket decision is correct.

They also check whether a ball has bounced before crossing the boundary to decide between scores of four or six in tight situations and whether a fielder has stopped a ball before the boundary without touching the boundary line or rope with any part of their body whilst they are in possession of the ball. If the fielder oversteps the boundary whilst holding onto the ball, a four is scored. At junior levels where such technology is not available, the umpires are solely responsible for all these decisions.

Third umpires and referees have the benefit of slow motion TV replays, and computer-generated prediction systems such as Hawk-Eye, Snicko or the Snickometer and Hot-Spot technology. I give some more information on Hawk-Eye on page 79, but I can explain here that the Snickometer is a sound recording device that picks up changes in sound (from the stump microphone) as the batsman hits the ball (or not, as the case may be). Sound visuals are generated that show if the ball has been struck or not and this aids decision making on LBW and catch decisions.

The Hot-Spot system picks up the spot on the bat where the ball just hit, using thermal imaging. It shows up as a white spot on a grey bat when shown on the TV, but clearly demonstrates if the bat has hit the ball or not. All this technology improves decision making for umpires and contentious decisions are generally avoided at Test level these days, thanks to these high tech developments. However not all Test sides use these review systems, instead trusting their umpires to make decisions without technological intervention.

Once the toss has taken place, the majority of the team that has chosen to bat (or has been put in to bat by the opposition) will leave the field and settle themselves down near the pavilion. Two of the batting team will put on batting pads and other protective padding and headgear, pick up a bat each and go out to the wicket to start their team's innings.

One of the umpires will go to stand near the square leg fielder – to one side of the batsman's wicket – so he can judge when the wicket is broken and whether a batsman is out. The other umpire will stand behind the opposite (non-striker's) wicket so he can judge the bowler's action and whether no-balls are being bowled and make leg-before-wicket decisions. Both umpires are responsible for checking fours and sixes and have to agree on wickets taken. At the end of each over they will swop roles, the square leg umpire moving in behind the non-striking batsman at his end of the pitch and the other umpire moving out to square leg.

You will also notice them moving position if a left-handed batsman comes on strike; the fielders will also swop over to the other side of the field to cope with his natural batting line.

Just for further clarification, the end of the pitch from which the bowler delivers the ball is known as the bowler's end. The opposite end is the batsman's end or the wicket-keeper's end.

Every time the ball is bowled, the fielders standing around the circle will move in towards the pitch no matter where on the field they stand. It's as if this action of moving forwards gets them into a heightened level of concentration ready to catch any balls that may come their way. Of course the close fielders are already standing close enough and don't need to move.

The captain of the fielding team spreads his fielders around the pitch and two of their number have specific roles: one is the bowler and the other is the wicket-keeper. The latter is the player wearing special leg pads and gloves who stands or crouches behind the wicket at one end of the pitch. I mentioned earlier that wicket-keeper's pads are generally shorter than batsmen's pads and the gloves have webbing between the thumb and first finger only, to assist them in catching fast-moving balls. They are not allowed to have webbing between the other fingers on their gloves.

It is the wicket-keeper's job to stop the ball that has been bowled by the bowler to make sure it doesn't go too far past the stumps. If he performs his role well he can save his teammates considerable time and energy by saving other fielders from having to chase balls which have been bowled past the batsman. In addition the wicket-keeper catches balls that glance off the bat, dismissing the batsman in the process, and he guards the stumps to ensure that balls being thrown in from the field do not go past the wicket for overthrows.

Young wicket-keepers, however, have not usually honed their skills sufficiently to cope with the vagaries of their peers' bowling techniques (in other words the young bowlers are frequently unable to bowl in a straight line at a regular point on the pitch). As a result, many badly bowled balls will evade the wicket-keeper's grasp and have to be chased by his teammates down to the boundary (this happens most often when a young fast bowler is at work).

The other specialists in the fielding team are the bowlers. In the next chapter you will find a description of the various types of bowler, which I hope you will find useful. They are usually described according to the speed with which they attack the opposition – fast, slow, medium and so on – but there are various other descriptions which are obviously designed to baffle any new cricket supporter.

The umpire indicates a no-ball.

As I explained earlier, the bowler bowls the ball to the batsmen in set periods called overs. Each over consists of six legal balls being bowled to one end of the pitch. Once the six balls have been bowled, the bowling changes ends and another bowler comes on to bowl from the opposite end of the pitch. This means that if a batsman does not succeed in scoring any runs during a particular over, he will not initially have to face the next one. Equally, if a very good batsman is playing with a poorer player, he can attempt to score an odd number of runs in an over to ensure that he faces more balls than his teammate. This obviously requires skill and intelligence if it's to work properly and the fielding side will do everything they can to keep the less talented batsman facing the bowler, as he will hopefully be easier to get out.

Sometimes you will notice that more than six balls are bowled during an over. This is because no-balls or wides have been called by the umpires and extra balls have to be bowled to make up for these bad deliveries.

Of course in limited-over cricket, the maximum number of overs each team is allowed to bowl is set beforehand, between thirty and forty being about the right number for an afternoon's school match. Once both teams have batted for the same number of overs, the scores are compared and the team with the highest number of runs wins the match. If the runs are even then the team with the least number of wickets lost will win. So a team scoring 120 for 7 (seven wickets lost) will beat a team scoring 120 for 9.

For a school cricket match, another method of limiting the overs is sometimes used: it may be agreed that the match will finish 20 overs after, say, six o'clock. The umpires and the scorers will make a note when six o'clock occurs and count the number of overs after that time, and will warn the teams when they are approaching their final overs.

Schools cricket that is played in this way, without strictly limited overs, can be very tedious and often frustrating to watch. If the first team to bat are not scoring particularly fast but their opposition are also failing to take wickets, they can stay at the crease until their captain is happy they have scored enough runs to give them a chance of beating the opposition, but he may also aim to give his opposition insufficient time to beat his team in the process, forcing a tie at worst!

As a result, the first team may stay in from 2.00 pm and continue after the tea break, which is usually taken around 4.15 pm. If they declare after five o'clock this can leave the opposition with only a couple of hours batting time compared with three hours or more used by the first team – not a fair match at all and definitely not cricket! Luckily it's rare these days and most inter-school games are 50-over matches; however, as I've already explained, long-standing annual fixtures played on a Saturday still use the no-limit system.

At the end of each over, the bowling swaps ends and, as I described earlier, the umpires will move so the umpire that stands close to the wicket is next to the bowler and the square leg umpire will stand at that position near the batsman on strike. The latter's position will vary depending on whether it's a right-handed or left-handed batsman playing and the fielders also move positions to match the new batsman on strike.

If there is a left-handed batsman playing, the fielders and umpires will need to move from one side of the pitch to the other every time he comes on strike, unless his fellow batsman is also a left-hander which can lengthen the time taken for each over considerably.

Batting and getting out (losing a wicket)

Batsmen arriving at the crease spend some time establishing their batting position. They will ask the umpire at the other end of the pitch to advise when their bat is in line with the middle or leg stump and mark the pitch in front of this line by raking the toe of their bat across the pitch. It can take some time before they actually take guard, standing ready to receive their first ball. I give full details of the shots employed by batsmen from page 108.

There are several ways in which a batsman can be out or lose his wicket.

1. The first is being bowled out. The bowler succeeds in getting the ball past the batsman and it knocks a bail or both bails off the stumps and in the most spectacular dismissals, the stumps are knocked out of the ground too.

    If this happens the fielders will rush over to congratulate the bowler and pat him on the back whilst the dejected batsman makes his way back to the pavilion, to be replaced by another member of his team. As the batsmen pass, words are frequently exchanged with the departing player; this may include him giving his team mate guidance on how to avoid a similar fate when playing against that particular bowler.

2. The second way to lose your wicket, and the simplest for the watcher to appreciate, is being caught out. The batsman hits the ball into the air off his bat, hand or gloves and one of the fielders catches it before it hits the ground.

    The rest of the team standing close by will rush towards the fielder who has caught the ball to congratulate him. They will also include the bowler in the celebrations as he gets the wicket credited to his score too. The kissing, hugging and elaborate celebrations of professional football players are not encouraged, but pats on the back and occasional hugs are seen, as well as much American-style high-five slapping of hands. In the past this would have been mistaken for players playing pat-a-cake but such sporting celebrations have become universal in the 21st century.

3. The third and perhaps most contentious way of losing a wicket, is being out leg before wicket or LBW. The ball must strike the batsman anywhere except on his bat, hands or gloves in such a way that if the ball had continued to travel through without interference, it would have knocked the bails off the stumps. The leg before wicket law is to cricket what the offside rule is to football (i.e. very confusing to the newcomer).

    The batsman is much less likely to be out leg before wicket if he has moved well forward in his stroke play and his front foot (the foot placed farthest towards the other end of the pitch) is well outside the crease. The decision process involved in ensuring that a player is fairly given out LBW is far too complicated for a simple explanation, but I'll do my best.

The umpire cannot give the batsman out if:

a) the ball pitches on the pitch outside the line of leg stump, regardless of whether or not the ball would have gone on to hit the stumps,

b) the ball hits the bat or the hand holding the bat before it strikes the pad,

c) the batsman is struck on the pad outside the line of off stump having made a genuine attempt to hit the ball and

d) the bowler has bowled a no-ball.

Action d is the most important part of the dismissal decision-making process; if the bowler has bowled a no-ball there is no way the batsman can be out, so that's the first thing the umpire at the bowler's end of the pitch (who is the umpire responsible for this decision) has to confirm.

Then action a is the next most important aspect of the decision. At Test matches the TV recordings include the Hawk-Eye system (also used in Grand Slam tennis and top-flight football matches) to review contentious LBW decisions, along with information from the Hot-Spot and Snickometer systems. Either the umpires or the teams themselves can request a review, although the latter are limited to two unsuccessful reviews in each innings for each team.

The third umpire can then review the Hawk-Eye computer-generated prediction and advise his colleagues on whether to give the batsman out or not. The slow-motion reviews are especially useful for showing if the ball landed outside leg or off stump. The Hawk-Eye system has an accuracy of within 3.6 mm, which is good but not perfect, so it does come in for criticism over decisions made using it from time to time and some international teams are still refusing to use it in Test matches.

Provided actions *a* through *d* are satisfied, the batsman will be out if he does not make any attempt to hit the ball – regardless of where he is hit – as long as the ball is going on to hit the stumps. In theory this means a batsman could be given out LBW if he's hit on the helmet, but this is very unlikely to happen.

The one absolute requirement for an LBW decision to be taken is that one member of the fielding team (often the bowler or wicket-keeper) should shout loudly 'Howzzat!' (or How was that?) to the umpire to claim the wicket. This is called making an appeal. If there here is no appeal, the umpire cannot give the batsman out LBW.

At the very early stages of cricket (such as the first proper match) it is not unheard-of for a young team to get a player out LBW but not know to appeal, and therefore the batsman gets to remain at the crease.

Needless to say they learn this lesson extremely rapidly and soon shouts of 'Howzzat' will resound around the field at regular intervals whether the batsman could be out or not. Enthusiastic young cricketers will need to learn to control the urge to yell for every ball bowled, however, as this could result in penalties.

Generally the fielders will not rush to congratulate the bowler immediately after requesting an LBW, since they have to wait for the umpire's decision. If the batsman is out, the umpire signifies this by raising his index finger to shoulder level or above and pointing his hand skywards, a little like an adult wagging his finger at a naughty child. Once a positive decision has been made, however, the bowler will receive the usual plaudits from his team.

It can be extremely difficult for the umpire to tell exactly whether or not the ball would have hit the stumps and at schools level they will tend take the side of the batsmen (it has been known for school umpires to be especially lenient to their own team but this is not generally what happens). However, this may well be the first experience children get of the potential inequities of umpiring and it takes great strength of character on their part not to object too vociferously if they believe the batsman should have been given out but the umpire disagrees. With the addition of the Spirit of the Game to cricket's laws since 2000 this situation has undoubtedly improved and I'm sure schools matches are being umpired totally impartially by umpires regardless of their affiliation nowadays.

In the past, a poor decision would often lead to much muttering under the breath and shaking of heads from the fielders. Comments on the quality of the umpire's eyesight and his need for a visit to the nearest optician should, however, be avoided. Good teaching staff and coaches will always be fair to both sides and it is hoped that the children will learn to accept all umpires' decisions in good faith. The umpire is only human (despite some of the comments you may hear to the contrary) and he can be right or wrong in equal measure. Learning to accept his decision as final with good grace is another part of the character-building nature of team sport which we should all seek to encourage in our youngsters.

The Spirit of the Game is such an important development that I have chosen to reproduce it in full later in this book. If you are a new cricketer, wanting to learn more about the game, this is essential reading; for the new supporter it will give you an idea of how vital the spirit of good sportsmanship is to the game of cricket. The familiar phrase 'that's just not cricket' refers to the game's long-held attitude to fair play and a lack of gamesmanship; anything that's 'not cricket' is probably unfair or demonstrates a degree of mean spirit and bad sportsmanship that the game is keen to exclude.

Now, returning to the ways a batsman can get out . . .

4. The fourth way to get out is to be stumped. If the batsman strays outside the crease in front of his stumps because he has just tried to hit the ball, the wicket-keeper can knock the bails off the stumps with the ball in his hand, and the batsman will be out if he is still outside the crease at the moment the bails are removed. The umpire standing at square leg (see the diagram on p. 101) is responsible for making this decision. The third umpire will also help these decisions if they are disputed at first-class matches.

5. The fifth way a batsman can be out is to be run out. In order to score runs, the batsmen are required to change ends and run down the pitch between the two wickets. Once their bat, or indeed any part of their body, touches the ground inside the crease at the opposite end and they remain behind that crease they cannot be run out.

However, if they are in the middle of the pitch and the bails are knocked from the stumps, either by the wicket-keeper or another player with the ball in his hands, or directly by the ball being thrown by a fielder at the stumps, then the stranded batsman nearest those stumps will be out. The batsman cannot be out if either a foot or his bat are on the ground inside the crease. Similar rules apply before a run begins, so you will often see players going through major contortions as they prepare to run down the pitch, with their body facing forwards and legs set to spring, one foot placed firmly behind the crease or their batting arm stretched behind their back with the bat placed firmly on the ground inside the crease.

When batsmen are about to run, the one who can see the direction of travel of the ball best will call out to say if the run is safe or not. If his opposite number countermands this call he must do so immediately and firmly, otherwise one of them will set off down the pitch and risk being run out. The standard calls are 'yes' or 'no'. If the decision can't be made until later – perhaps depending on the efficiency of a fielder – the initial call will be 'wait' or 'waiting' and once the fielder's action is clear, this will be clarified by a standard yes or no call.

Because it is very difficult for the umpires to tell if the batsman has reached the crease before the ball hits the stumps, run outs and stumpings are often controversial, and this was the major driving factor behind the introduction of the third umpire at international level. At junior levels umpires are frequently accused of getting these important decisions wrong by the players in the batting team, who can have the benefit of a good view albeit from the edge of the cricket ground!

Nevertheless, in common with all other team sports, the umpire's decision is final and all junior players are trained to leave the wicket immediately they have been told by the umpire they are out – without argument or dissent – exactly as the Spirit of the Game requires. Remember in the event of any doubt, the umpire will always give the benefit of the doubt to the batsman rather than the fielding team.

Finally, there are a few other ways in which a batsman can get out which are extremely rare, although you should be aware they exist.

6. If the batsman himself hits his wicket – either with his bat or body – and the bails are dislodged, he is out. This is also the case if part of his clothing or equipment falls onto the wicket and if part of his bat breaks off and goes onto the wicket too. Hitting the wicket sometimes occurs when a batsman has unbalanced himself, usually playing at a ball off the back foot, and topples backwards towards the wicket.

Occasionally you will see batsmen trying to leap over the stumps rather than hit them, but since high jumping or hurdling are not an integral part of cricket training, and the pads definitely get in the way, they are not usually successful in clearing the wicket in this way and are frequently out. Very occasionally if the batsman is standing close to the wicket and the backlift of his bat is too great he can hit the wicket with his bat as he aims for a hefty shot. Once again he will be out if he breaks the wicket.

7. If a batsman deliberately hits the ball twice he will also be dismissed, unless he is attempting to stop the ball continuing toward his wicket which he is allowed to do. However, a junior batsman might just automatically hit at the ball to give it back to the fielders, as he would in practice sessions, and this would result in him losing his wicket if he had already hit the ball once. If play has obviously halted, ready for the ball to be returned the bowler, no umpire will give a player out if

he returned the ball to the other team out of courtesy, but it's a law that all new players have to learn.

8. Another way a batsman can be dismissed is if he obstructs the fielding team. If he deliberately prevents a fielder from getting to the ball or throwing it at the stumps, he is deemed to be obstructing the field and will be given out. He can also be out if he picks the ball up, perhaps to give it back to the other side, if he has not previously asked their permission to do this.

9. And last of all, a batsman can actually be timed out if he is believed to be spending too long preparing himself to face the attacking bowler following the fall of a wicket. This is obviously designed to speed up matches but it is a very unusual law and is unlikely to be applied at junior or schools level. Under the laws, the incoming batsman has to reach the crease within 3 minutes of the previous wicket falling.

If your youngsters are cricketers, they will soon learn to play as part of a team, to help their teammates and to accept decisions from umpires (even when they're incorrect) and all these things can be taken into adulthood as useful tools. They will also learn to accept blame when they miss the wicket with a bad throw or when they lose their own wicket on the first ball they face (being out before you score is known as being out for a duck and getting out on the first ball counts as a golden duck). All these vicissitudes will help them become stronger, more self-confident people in general life.

We all have experience of working with someone whose opinion we believe is wrong, but know when (and when not) to point this out; just one of the benefits of having played team games in our youth perhaps.

Hopefully you now have a feel for the main elements that make up a cricket match, so let's give you more detail on the individual skills involved in making a good cricket team. I would say 'making a first-class cricket team' but in cricket that has a distinct meaning, referring specifically to county and Test cricketers. In all parts of the world the first-class teams are considered the cream of the country's cricketers. You will find lists of first-class teams available online for all major cricketing nations. We've provided a link to the England first-class county listing at the back of the book in our links section. In England there are minor counties too, who also play 3-day matches throughout the season, as well as their own Twenty20 tournaments.

The players and their skills

Bowlers

Bowlers are defined by the speed at which they deliver the ball. There are two main divisions: pace bowlers (those who bowl fast) and spin bowlers (those who bowl much slower). A typical fast delivery has a speed in the range of 137-153 km/h (85-95 mph), but your young player will only bowl at 30-40 km/h.

You may have heard of some of the fastest bowlers at international level where famous names are in the list of the top 10 fastest bowlers of all time:

Name	Country played for	Fastest time recorded
Lasith Malinga	Sri Lanka	155.7 km/h
Dale Steyn	South Africa	155.7 km/h
Shane Bond	New Zealand	156.4 km/h
Mohammad Sami	Pakistan	156.4 km/h
Mitchell Johnson	Australia	156.8 km/h
Fidel Edwards	West Indies	157.7 km/h
Andy Roberts	West Indies	159.5 km/h
Jeff(rey) Thompson	Australia	160.4 km/h
Shaun Tait	Australia	161.1 km/h
Brett Lee	Australia	161.1 km/h
Shoaib Akhtar	Pakistan	161.3 km/h

For those of you who only think in miles per hour, Shoaib Akhtar's record is the equivalent of 100.2 mph. Current England pace bowlers you may have heard of include Steven Finn, Stuart Broad and Jimmy Anderson.

Even an averagely fast bowler has to be very fit, since he not only has the longest run-up of all the bowlers but he also delivers the ball much faster than the others. This requires speed from the run-up being combined with a very fast overarm or round arm action. Controversy sometimes accompanies new bowlers at international level, never more so than for Lasith Malinga of Sri Lanka, whose round arm technique was initially much criticised and has earned him the nickname 'Malinga the slinger'.

Check this website:
>> http://in.answers.yahoo.com/question/
   index?qid=20090507215814AAgAcYW

for an explanation of why his action passed the scrutiny of the ICC. It sometimes seems the bowling arm of pace bowlers windmills around prior to bowling the ball down the pitch at the batsman. As you can see from the top ten table, top-flight bowlers are all capable of bowling the ball at over 90 mph on a regular basis.

It is these bowlers that are capable of delivering a ball short of a length that will bounce high and may surprise a batsman. These balls are known as bouncers. Balls that are bowled straight at the batsman's head without bouncing are called beamers; they are illegal and will result in a no-ball being called. However, they can unsettle a new or even a settled batsman and from a bowler's point of view may be worth incurring a no-ball call and the extra ball he'll need to bowl in that over when the following ball might get an unsettled batsman out.

Obviously schoolchildren will not attain such speeds, generally only bowling up to 40 mph when learning, but by their senior years the fastest are getting close to these speeds and are duly feared by their opposition. However once they are bowling at these sorts of speeds, they need to be careful where they finish their bowling action. There is a protected area or danger area that forms the central portion of the pitch; it is a rectangle running down the middle of the pitch, two feet wide and beginning five feet from each popping crease. Under the laws of cricket, a bowler must avoid running on this area during his follow-through after delivering the ball.

If a bowler runs on the protected area, an umpire will issue a warning to the bowler and to his team captain. The umpire issues a second and final warning if the bowler transgresses again. On the third offence, the umpire will instruct the fielding captain to remove that bowler from the attack and he won't be allowed to bowl again for the remainder of that innings. This sanction is usually sufficient for most bowlers to mend their ways (and change their running trajectory) after the first warning is issued.

This area is protected in this way because the ball normally bounces on the pitch within this region, and if it is scuffed or damaged by the bowler's footmarks it can give an unfair advantage to the bowling side.

This rule does not prevent the bowler or any other fielder from running onto the protected area in an effort to field the ball; it only applies to the uninterrupted follow-through after the bowler has bowled the ball.

England's James (Jimmy) Anderson and Steven Finn are considered fast-medium bowlers, as was the great all-rounder Sir Ian Botham. These bowlers use a similar long run-up but can't quite match their super-fast bowling peers for speed. They might not be super fast, but they can swing the ball in the air (swing bowling) and hit the seam to make the ball bounce at odd angles to bamboozle the batsman (seam bowling). All fast bowlers use swing or seam to affect the trajectory of the ball, and the very best can use both.

Swing bowlers use positioning of the seam and differing surfaces of the ball to swing it in flight. Historically, Wasim Akram and Waqar Younis of Pakistan and Glenn McGrath of Australia were probably the best-known proponents of this form of bowling.

Medium pace bowlers may use slightly shorter run-ups but are still capable of bowling a good fast ball. It's their ability to swing the ball that distinguishes them, and their accuracy is generally better than that of out-and-out fast bowlers.

See my table below that divides up the speed of all bowlers quite neatly:

Type	km/h	mph
Fast	≥ 142	≥ 89
Fast-medium	130-141	81-88
Medium-fast	120-129	75-80
Medium	96-119	60-74
Slow bowling	< 96	< 60

All bowlers are capable of using the seam that binds the leather ball to influence the way the ball travels through the air or bounces off the ground. The ball may swing in the air, especially when it is new and the weather conditions are just right. The application of shine to one side of the ball, whilst leaving the other side matte or even rough will also make the ball swing in the air. High-speed swing bowling at its best results in the ball travelling through the air in a banana-like trajectory. Balls can swing out or in depending on their path to the wicket.

You will frequently see bowlers (and indeed their teammates) busily rubbing the ball on their trousers to put shine on one side of the ball, whilst keeping the other side rough. Pity the mother whose child discovers this activity early in his career, since the red dye on leather cricket balls is only too happy to transfer itself to their trousers, which will then need extra laundry treatment to return them to their former pristine glory.

If you are wondering how swing is achieved, the technique involved is actually quite complicated and fascinating; an outswinger is bowled by holding the cricket ball with the seam at an angle and the first two fingers running along either side of the seam. Once the ball has started to wear and been polished so that one side is rougher than the other, the rough side is placed on the left (as seen from the bowler's viewpoint). Then, when the bowler delivers the ball, he will angle the seam so that it points slightly to the left as well, and release the ball so the seam rotates along that rotational axis. The angle of the seam to the direction of motion produces an aerofoil effect as the ball moves through the air, pushing it to the left. This is enhanced by differential air pressure caused by the movement of air over the rough and smooth surfaces, which also tends to push the ball to the left. As a result the ball curves, or swings, to the left.

From a right-handed batsman's point of view, the swing is away from his body towards his right (i.e. towards the off-side). This swing away from the body is the source of the name outswinger. To a left-handed batsman, the same ball will swing in towards the body and towards the leg side, which from a technical point of view makes the outswinger now an inswinger.

Outswingers are considered to be one of the more difficult fast deliveries for a right-handed batsman to play. This is because the ball moves away from his body which means that any miscalculation on his part can result in an outside edge off the bat and a catch going to the wicket-keeper or the slips fielders.

For the natural inswinger, the ball is bowled by holding the cricket ball with the seam vertical and the first two fingers slightly across the seam so that it is angled a little to the leg side (to the right from the bowler's viewpoint) with the rough side of the ball on the leg side. The ball is then placed on the pad of the thumb. This thumb locks the wrist in a position inclined to the leg side. When the ball is bowled the seam will be angled so that it points slightly to the leg side. To help achieve this position the bowler's arm needs to be near vertical, brushing close to his ear. At release, the wrist remains cocked, which should put backspin on the ball along the line of the seam. The angle of the seam to the direction of motion again produces an aerofoil effect as the ball moves through the air, this time pushing it to the leg side. Again differential air pressure plays its part and the ball will curve, or swing, in towards the batsman.

Another delivery in the fast bowler's arsenal is the full toss, when the ball is delivered straight towards the batsman without bouncing. It must not arrive too high or it will be a beamer and will result in a no-ball being called, but as long as it arrives around waist height it will be legal. If the batsman sees a full toss coming, he can prepare to hook or pull the ball far and high, but for the fast bowler it's one of his scary balls that can unsettle a batsman.

If the bowler can manage to bowl in such a way that the ball lands on the seam when it hits the ground, the ball will then deviate in one direction or another – just to confuse the batsman – and this is called seam bowling.

Balls that land in this way are termed leg-cutter or off-cutter depending on their trajectory; they are bowled at medium pace with a spinner's wrist action which makes the ball turn just like a standard spinner's delivery. Medium-pace bowlers vary the pace at which they bowl, and they tend to use a shorter run-up, which means they get through their overs quicker than fast bowlers, which can be useful at international level where overs per day are counted and, as I explained earlier, a team can be penalised if they don't complete sufficient overs during a day's cricket.

The medium-pace bowler is therefore a very useful addition to the team as he can vary speed from slow to medium-fast, add swing and seaming to the ball's trajectory and bamboozle batsmen accordingly.

The second main bowling technique used in cricket is *spin bowling*. This involves delivering the ball at a much slower pace. The spin bowler can spin the ball as it flies through the air, so that when it bounces off the pitch near the batsman it goes off at an oblique angle instead of continuing in a straight line (the only exception to this being when a bowler is using top spin which does go straight on towards the wicket). There are two main actions that cause the spin: use of the wrist and the fingers.

Wrist spinners

As the name suggests, wrist spinners use their wrists to spin the ball. A right-handed wrist spinner is known as a leg spinner, and he bowls leg-breaks. A leg-break moves from right to left from the bowler's point of view, or from the leg-side to the off-side for a right-handed batsman. Hopefully you have heard of Shane Warne of Australia and Anil Kumble of India, two of the most successful bowlers of spin in Test cricket. While a normal leg-break spins from the leg to the off side, away from a right-handed batsman, a googly spins the other way moving towards the batsman. It's a sort of reverse leg-break, but not an off-break because it's bowled by a wrist spinner not a finger spinner. Yes I know this is really confusing, but bear with me. The googly is a major weapon in the arsenal of a leg-spin bowler, and can be one of the bowler's most effective wicket-taking balls. It is used infrequently, because its effectiveness comes mostly from its surprise value.

Wrist spinners are also capable of delivering balls with top spin and balls called sliders. Whereas a top-spinner is released with the thumb facing the batsman, a slider is bowled with the thumb facing the bowler. On release the wrist and ring finger work to put backspin into the ball. A top-spinner tends to dip more quickly and bounce higher than a normal delivery. The slider does the opposite; it floats to a fuller length and bounces less than the batsman might expect.

Typically these balls head towards the batsman with a scrambled or wobbling seam (i.e. the ball is not spinning in the direction of the seam, so the seam direction is not constant, unlike in conventional spin bowling). This has less effect on the flight and bounce but the mere absence of traditional leg spin might just deceive the batsman. The slider can be bowled with a mixture of side spin and backspin. For the batsman, this has the effect of making the ball harder to differentiate from the leg-break, without reducing the mechanical effects caused by the backspin. It may therefore either skid straight on or sometimes it may turn a small amount just to keep the batsman confused.

It was Shane Warne's use of the delivery in the 2005 Ashes series that brought this variation back into public consciousness for the first time really since the 1960s and although there is often a good deal of confusion on the subject, the slider is also thought to be more or less identical to the zooter. Cricketers are certainly imaginative when it comes to naming a bowler's different deliveries. There is also a leg-break ball called a flipper, which is similar and you'll find an explanation in the weblinks at the back of the book.

It should also be noted that bowlers who employ finger spin can bowl an identical ball, which comes out of the front of their hand with backspin present. These are not, however, called sliders, and are described as back-spinners and, more recently, they have been called a teesra instead.

Left-handed wrist spinners are rare and are called chinaman bowlers. They are named after a left-handed wrist spinner of Chinese descent named Ellis Achong who played for the West Indies international team. A ball delivered in this way will spin from the off-side towards the leg side for a right-handed batsman.

Finger spinners

As the name suggests, they use their fingers to rotate the ball. A right-arm finger spinner is also known as an off-spinner and they bowl off-breaks. The ball appears to move just like a chinaman ball, and Muttiah Muralitharan of Sri Lanka and England's Graeme Swann are two of the most successful current proponents of this style of bowling. Saqlain Mushtaq of Pakistan has also invented a new delivery called a doosra. It is bowled with almost exactly the same action as the off-break, but it spins like a leg-break or goes straight on in line with the angle of the delivery. It has become one of the most effective deliveries in the spin bowler's armoury and is used by several other international stars now.

Most left-handed slow bowlers are finger spinners, hence the rarity of chinaman bowlers. As a result this style has no fixed name and is merely known as slow left-arm orthodox bowling. Their balls turn like leg-breaks from leg to off and Pakistan's Shaeed Ajmal and New Zealand's Daniel Vettori are famous for this style of bowling.

Then there are pure slow bowlers. They bowl slowly but don't employ spin of any sort. They rarely make it into Test sides, as without spin, their hit rates are rather low but, if they are truly accurate in line and length and have a good variation of speed, they can prevent runs from being scored. New Zealand's Chris Harris is a current player of note.

Finally there are all-round bowlers. A very rare breed indeed, all-round bowlers are equally skilled at more than one type of bowling, Sir Garfield (Gary) Sobers, being the most famous. He was capable of bowling left-arm fast-medium, left-arm orthodox and chinaman style.

There are also batsmen who have a part-time duty of bowling. Some of these are known as partnership breakers as they have an ability to get a good or settled player out; Joe Root of England is such a player in the current era.

True all-rounders like Gary Sobers and Sir Ian Botham are rare; they can bowl and bat equally well and can be relied on to pull their team out of trouble. Freddie Flintoff was another all-rounder whose ability to save or win a game has made him a legend in English cricket. Across the world Jacques Kallis of South Africa, Imran Khan of Pakistan and Richard Hadlee of Australia also make it into the top ten.

There are two other deliveries of the ball that all bowlers are capable of bowling: the yorker and the full toss. I mentioned the latter earlier on; it's aimed straight at the batsman, aiming to hit near the top of his bat. It travels the full length of the pitch without bouncing and is difficult to handle if bowled at speed, and can encourage a batsman to hit out if bowled by a spin bowler. It frequently leads to the batsman being caught out as a result. The yorker is also designed to travel the full length of the pitch, landing right at the batsman's feet, almost right up against the stumps, in the area described by commentators as the block hole, which makes it very difficult to block and prevent the wicket or the batsman's pads from being hit.

Is it any wonder that early bowling skills are somewhat haphazard? The slower bowlers can rarely get into too much trouble at the outset. They have to learn to bowl the full length of the pitch (farther for an eight-year-old than it seems to an adult), and they also need to learn how to bowl on the same path on a regular basis, again not as easy as it sounds with the overarm action, but once they have mastered this they can then add the use of spin to their repertoire.

Fast bowlers, however, can get into all sorts of trouble, as I have already suggested. They take longer to learn how to bowl at the same place on the pitch every time; given the fast run-up and fast overarm action required, this is not at all surprising. In addition, because of the long run-up they have difficulty in not over-stepping the crease as they bowl and are responsible for more no-ball calls than their slower counterparts. In the early stages of a fast bowler's career he will be the chap who ends up bowling more than six balls an over on a regular basis and he will rapidly get removed from the bowling attack if he cannot get his run-up right after a couple of overs.

Regrettably, it can take three or four overs for him to adjust his run-up to avoid no-balls. The captain's frustration at the extra runs being awarded to the opposition can frequently prevent a fast bowler from ever getting it right; his captain will give him his chance but only for two or three overs each time so the poor bowler never quite sorts it all out. The habit of using nets for bowling practice rather than the proper pitch does not help this problem, and fast bowlers frequently complain that they never get a chance to truly establish the length of their run up in a match situation before the season starts.

Bowlers usually deliver the ball from the side of the wicket nearest their bowling arm (i.e. over the wicket). However they can also bowl round the wicket. This allows slow bowlers in particular to alter the angle of delivery to confuse the batsmen. It's easy to tell which side they are bowling. For a right-handed bowler, if the stumps are behind him as he bowls, then the bowler is bowling round the wicket (see the pitch diagram on page 48). The umpire will also advise the batsman what style of bowling to expect, calling out 'right-arm over' or 'left-arm round' for instance.

An unusual addition to the cricketers' armoury was the introduction of zinc-based sun creams in the 1980s. Facial adornments have been part of cricket since the early days of WG Grace and his famous whiskers, which were followed by the impressive moustache of Mervyn Hughes of Australia and added to by England's Bob Willis's 70s mop of hair, and in the 21st century Ryan Sidebottom's long curly locks. The new sun cream allowed players to war-paint their faces and this obviously increased a fast bowler's aggressive stance at the start of his run-up. They even seem to use it regardless of the weather these days, just like war paint.

So, understand all of this if you dare. Bowling is no simple matter. All manner of styles, speeds and abilities are required. All you need to know is that if your youngster is a spin bowler, they will not just be throwing the ball down the pitch (indeed throwing the ball with a bent arm that straightens results in a no-ball being called!) but will be applying every law of science they can muster to bamboozle the batsman at the opposite end of the pitch.

I hope this round-up of bowling styles has helped to clarify in your mind what it is that bowlers do and has not confused you with too much detail. Obviously you can always learn more online. There are many good reference websites that explain the intricacies of the doosra, the flipper, the teesra and the googly if you're still confused (and I certainly won't blame you if you are).

Fielding positions

For the newcomer to this sport, this must be the most confusing part of cricket. It is certainly the aspect that takes boys and girls the longest to learn, for placing a field is a skill that many captains seem to struggle with, even at senior level. Doing a good job at junior level must be even harder, especially when your teammates don't even know where the positions you want them to stand in are located yet. This results in a great deal of arm waving and finger pointing until the fielders take up the correct positions on the field.

Look at the diagram on the next page for the exact placing of fielders. As the diagram on page 23 showed, the field is divided into three areas: the close infield (close to the batsman); the infield (the next level away from the batsman); and the outfield (the area closer to the boundary). You will also see the field is divided down the pitch between the leg (or on) side and the offside.

As the fielding side only has nine players to spread around the field (because the bowlers and wicket-keeper have specific functions), great skill is needed to place fielders where they will take catches and prevent runs.

Slips (first, second and third, etc.)

In theory there is no limit to the number of slip fielders you can place but putting in more than three is generally considered to be self-defeating as this would leave the rest of the ground bereft of fielders and the batsman would soon score vast numbers of runs in other areas of the ground.

The job of the slip fielders is to catch balls which just touch the bat and slip off towards the off-side (these are also called snicks or edges). The slips cordon are thought of as great heroes since it is their spectacular diving or leaping catches that can dismiss some of the best batsmen; however, their positions close up to the batsman can also be considered quite dangerous and require courageous players to fill them. There is also a leg slip position on the other side of the wicket which gets used when

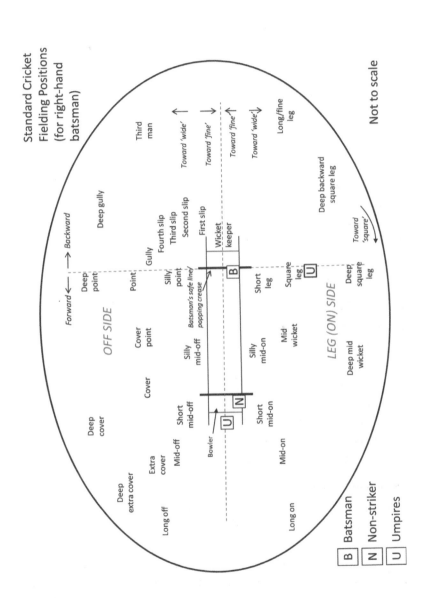

Standard Cricket Fielding Positions (for right-hand batsman)

Not to scale

OFF SIDE

LEG (ON) SIDE

Forward ← → Backward

Third man

Toward 'wide'
Toward 'fine'
Toward 'fine'
Toward 'wide'

Long/fine leg

Deep gully

Gully

Deep backward square leg

Fourth slip
Third slip
Second slip
First slip

Wicket keeper

Toward 'square'

Deep point

Point

Silly point

Batsman's safe line/ popping crease

Short leg

Square leg

Deep square leg

Cover point

Silly mid-off

Mid wicket

Cover

Silly mid-on

Deep mid wicket

Short mid-off

Mid-off

Short mid-on

Deep cover

Bowler

Extra cover

Deep extra cover

Long off

Mid-on

Long on

B Batsman

N Non-striker

U Umpires

an aggressively attacking field is being set around a batsman. Slips swop over to the other side of the wicket when a left-handed batsman comes to the crease, of course.

For a right-handed batsman, first slip stands to the side of and about a foot behind the wicket-keeper, because balls heading off at an angle go faster than straight balls. The second and third slips stand two to three feet away (sometimes more) from each other in an arc on the offside of the batsman.

Gully

This has nothing to do with being close to the area where seagulls land on the grass, although they do frequent cricket pitches around the country and can cause problems. It is just a position in line with the slips but slightly farther away from the wicket. The gully fielder is placed here to catch difficult edges and shoulder-height catches. If your little one fields here they will need to be a good catcher of a speeding cricket ball.

Mid-wicket and cover point

Pretty dangerous places to stand, located at a central point between the two sets of stumps where many balls are hit, some with great ferocity. These players are responsible for running out more batsmen than all the other fielders put together (except for the wicket-keeper of course). Fielders here are really quite brave!

Silly mid-on

Given this name for a perfectly good reason – anyone in his right mind would never stand here. One good whack from the batsman could send the ball hurtling towards the fielder at a frightening speed and could cause irreparable damage to any part of his anatomy that is hit. These days fielders in this position regularly wear protective helmets and sometimes shin pads and a box.

Silly mid-off

Exactly the same position but on the other side of the batsman – slightly less dangerous but not a lot. There are several other silly positions in the field, including silly point. By now you'll have realised that silly positions are merely those that are even closer to the batsman than their normal counterparts – silly means very close to the bat.

You will be pleased to learn that there are special laws preventing younger players (those under 14 years of age) from standing too close to the batsman because of the danger involved. Whilst this will prevent your young son or daughter from getting any serious injury early on in their playing career, as soon as they get into a more senior team in the club or school this caution will cease and the danger positions will become part of playing the game. It definitely takes a brave cricketer to enjoy standing in these positions in the field.

Captains often field in the mid-off area as this is a good position where they are close enough to the bowler to pass on advice and encouragement. In addition to the silly mid-off position, there is also deep mid-off (which is usually three-quarters of the way toward the boundary) and long-off right out by the boundary rope. There are mid-on equivalents located on the other side of the batsman of course.

Long-leg

Nothing to do with the size of the field or the length of his legs but merely a description for a position to one side of the batsman (on the side of leg stump), the term *long* referring to the distance from the stumps. In other words, they stand very close to the boundary. Other boundary positions have the added word *deep* to indicate their position (for example, deep mid-wicket).

Short-leg

No, he's not the shortest player in the team, just one of the brave ones who stand on the same line from the wicket as long leg, but closer in.

This is another of the hero positions of the infield. Reactions for this player need to be extremely sharp and it is generally advised that they wear a helmet, box and shin guards! Fast balls will definitely be coming in their direction.

Short leg
and long leg

Fine-leg

Absolutely nothing to do with Chippendale furniture or fashion models, this position is found between square-leg and the line of the wickets. It comes in various forms (short fine-leg and deep fine-leg) but once they are really close to the wickets the position becomes a leg slip.

Square-leg

Again, nothing at all to do with the shape of the fielder's leg: they are merely standing on the leg side (the side of the leg stump) at right angles to the length of the pitch and in line with the batsman's stumps. This player has the pleasure of the second umpire's company throughout the game.

Other leg positions include deep square leg and backward square leg.

Third-man

Not a Graham Greene book character but a fielder who stands near the off-side boundary (deep third-man stands next to the boundary rope or fence). The position is located behind and to the side of the off stump. Third man is responsible for covering a large area of the pitch boundary, pretty much any ball that travels between slip and gully, and Test teams tend not to use a third man if they prefer to attack rather than defend.

Point

The final position we'll describe has nothing to do with pointing fingers, this position is merely placed half way between gully and cover at right angles to the length of the pitch and in line with the batsman's stumps, on the off-side. There is also a cover point position which is in between cover and point. And of course there's also the silly point position.

1. Wicketkeeper
2. Slip
3. Gully
4. Point
5. Cover
6. Mid-off
7. Bowler
8. Mid-on
9. Mid-wicket
10. Fine leg
11. Third man
B Batsman
U Umpire
○ Fielding circle

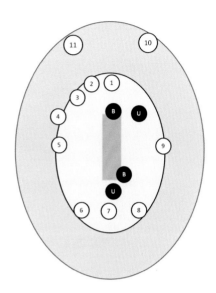

Here's an alternative view of a cricket pitch with the major fielding positions marked out. As it's less comprehensive than the previous diagram I hope it might help you to understand more about the names of places on the field. At junior level there is also a possible position between 10 and 11 above, called long-stop. This player provides support to the wicket-keeper when a fast bowler is bowling.

Fielding techniques

Fielders are taught early on in their training how to position their bodies to ensure balls don't get through to the boundary. This usually involves them dropping to one knee so they can put their hands in front of the bent leg and if the ball misses their hands their leg will still halt it.

Fielders also need to learn how to catch speeding cricket balls. They must always watch the ball all the way into their hands, using both hands cupped together rather than a single hand whenever possible. However, some of the most spectacular catches are made by leaping close fielders, including those in the slips, with outstretched single arms that seem to pull the ball out of the air as if by magic.

Learning how to catch the hard ball is one of the first lessons every cricketer will be taught. Softening the hands to allow a certain amount of follow through helps stop the ball from hurting you but also takes time to learn. Hard hands result in balls bouncing out of the catcher's grip and many wicket-taking opportunities are missed as a result.

Fielders near the boundary have to be very careful not to overstep the boundary line with the ball in their hand, which would automatically score four or six runs depending on whether the ball has bounced already or not. To avoid overstepping the line, they can slide spectacularly along the edge of the ground and either scoop the ball infield and then stand up and pick it up themselves or sweep the ball with one hand to a tracking fielder who can then throw it back towards the wicket. It can be a real team effort to stop a speeding ball from scoring a four.

Throwing accurately and fast over long distances, with a flick of the elbow to keep the ball low, is a real skill that all young cricketers will do well to master. The quicker the ball is returned to the wicket-keeper, the fewer runs will be conceded and more wickets are likely to tumble.

Batting techniques

For the purposes of these explanations I will assume the batsman is right-handed – obviously for a left-handed player all the shots played towards the on-side travel to the opposite side of the pitch.

In preparation to hit the oncoming ball, the batsman raises his bat behind him (using backlift), then swings it at the ball. If he swings hard and the bat continues on its way, it will follow through until it is raised above his head, forming a complete stroke (except when he is making a hook shot or check drive).

Here are a few names of strokes which you will hear about during cricket commentaries. This is by no means a complete list, but will give you a feel for the sorts of strokes than can be employed by the batsmen.

Drive

An attacking forward stroke which comes in a variety of styles: the cover drive, the off drive and the check drive (no, not a Scotsman's plaid but a swing of the bat which is checked or stopped before the full follow through). It is usually hit off a full or an over-pitched ball.

Pull and hook shots

These include the shots described as smashing it over the top. It's everyone's favourite shot – both cricketer and crowd.

The hook shot is all about hitting the ball hard so that it flies off to the left, sometimes behind the batsman, to the on-side of the field. Usually it is hit off a short-pitched ball with very little follow through of the bat. The batsman needs to hit the ball really hard, either along the ground or as high as possible to make sure it clears the fielders and hopefully scores either four or preferably six. The over-the-top description refers to going over the top of the infield to clear the close fielders before reaching the boundary – hopefully without interception en route. The pull is just a similar shot played off a delivery arriving around waist height.

The hook, being played to a shorter delivery which bounces between chest and head height, is the most difficult shot to control. It's very difficult to roll your wrists to keep the ball down while playing the hook, so the ball is likely to be in the air for several seconds. Wearing a helmet is definitely advisable for this shot, as it can easily go wrong and send the ball spinning off the bat straight towards the batsman's head. Quick footwork is also essential to get into the correct position to play the stroke.

Forward defensive

The raison d'être of the famed Geoffrey Boycott of England. No one has ever played the forward defensive quite so effectively or seemingly for so long in a match as the infamous Mr Boycott. For the spectator, it has to be the most boring shot ever developed (presumably hence its unpopularity in the modern game). In truth it's not so much a shot as a stroke.

It consists of placing the bat with the toe of the blade firmly planted in front of the pad and the handle held forward at an angle over the blade. Any ball that hits the bat is immediately stopped in its tracks and returned down the pitch towards the bowler at ground level. Although boring to watch, it is a very useful stroke for the new batsman at the crease until he gets his eye in and has ascertained the speed of the incoming balls. It's also essential for a Test batsman who is struggling to stay in against a heated bowling attack. So perhaps Mr Boycott was right after all; it may not be pretty but it's certainly effective.

It may also prove a frustration to bowlers, who may be tempted to bowl some wilder balls to make the batsman change his tactics, but over after over of forward defensive play will also tend to elicit a round of slow hand-clapping from a modern crowd weaned on a diet of Twenty20 and one-day cricket and potentially unaware of the psychological battle involved in a five-day Test match. The forward defensive can also be played with the bat off the ground, but at the identical angle. This copes with higher bouncing balls in an equally efficient (but sadly just as boring) manner. It is frequently described as a block in commentary, and the batsman is said to be blocking the ball.

The straight drive

This classic batting shot, usually played to a full-length delivery arriving on or just outside off stump, just requires the batsman to hit the ball back along the ground, down the pitch towards and past the bowler.

Tickle

Nothing to do with the Mr Men character thankfully. This is a stroke played behind point (see the diagram on page 106 for this position) on the off-side. It involves the batsman angling his bat against the ball as it hits the face of the bat, diverting its path away from the wicket and towards point.

Square cut

A ball hit square on the off-side. If bowlers give batsmen a short and wide delivery outside off stump, chances are they'll be hit for four, square of the wicket, using this shot. The square cut allows batsmen to free their arms and hit the ball with a cross bat, enabling them to get plenty of power on the shot. But they need to be careful, since although a square cut can bag plenty of runs, it can also lead to the batsman's downfall if he gets too confident, and he may be caught out unless his aim is spot on.

The square cut is quite a technical shot: the batsman's back foot moves back towards the stumps and across towards the line of the ball. He keeps his head still and rolls his wrists forwards to keep the ball down. The front shoulder should turn to the off-side as the bat is taken back. The bat is brought down and across, making contact with the ball at full arm extension. The player then follows through with the shot, leaving the weight on his back foot and the bat finishes over his front shoulder and behind his head. It's wonderful to watch it being played correctly.

Sweep shot

The sweep has become the favoured shot against spinners, and is often used by England's international batsmen. The batsman generally drops to one knee to play this shot. It is a cross-batted shot played behind square on the leg side to a delivery arriving on or around leg stump; hopefully that makes sense to you now. It should get past square leg in the field and although it's a relatively risky shot it's good fun to see in action. Batsmen also turn their bats around to hit the reverse sweep shot past their other shoulder.

Chip shot

A chip shot follows a gentle lob trajectory over infielders, allowing the batsman to get one or two runs. A chip shot rarely reaches the outfield; it is just lifted high enough to clear the close fielders to allow the batsmen to run.

In recent years a variation of this shot has arrived in the batsman's armoury; it's daring and dangerous, but spectacular when it's successful. It's the shot that chips the ball over the head of the wicket-keeper, much loved by England batsman Ian Bell and other top-flight batsmen around the world. Sadly it also results in dismissals when the batsman completely miscalculates the trajectory of the incoming ball, misses it completely and can be out LBW or bowled.

Playing off the front foot

A term to describe how the batsman is holding his body whilst batting. For a young player, batting off the front foot will mean you're an aggressive, pro-active batsman, although this is the stance adopted for playing the forward defensive stroke too. The front foot is, fairly obviously, the foot placed farthest down the pitch and pushed forward to balance the body while the arms swing the bat. Batsmen normally play off the front foot for full or over-pitched balls and off the back foot for short- or high-pitched balls that fly up at them from the pitch.

You will frequently hear commentators on TV and radio complaining: 'he's not moving his feet'. This criticism is because the best batsmen move their feet to adjust their stance to play their shots and non-movement of the feet can indicate a nervous, reticent or incompetent batsman.

Playing off the back foot

The reverse of playing off the front foot and sometimes the sign of an unsettled batsman. A junior batsman will not be well balanced when playing off the back foot and is usually playing defensively against high pitching balls. Bowlers, fast ones especially, take great delight in bowling balls that force the batsman to play off the back foot. It is, however, a technique that can be mastered, and many a fast bowler has been smashed all over the ground by a quality player, such as current England captain Alistair Cook, playing off his back foot.

An edge

Generally a bad shot but sometimes a lucky one – the batsman has really almost missed the ball when it comes off the edge of the bat. This frequently results in the batsman being caught out. Edges can be thick or thin, depending on how badly the batsman has missed his stroke. Thick edges make firm contact with the bat, thin ones just clip off the edge. Occasionally, however, they can work to the batsman's advantage and send a fast ball off at an odd angle that defeats the fielders, allowing runs to be scored. There's a very fine line between a tickle and an edge!

I hope you've found this round-up of cricket skills informative. Now let's move on to some practical advice for you as a supporter.

Here's a very neat diagram that shows you where the various shots in the batsman's armoury will travel – assume the batsman is standing facing the straight drive zone. You will see there is an area directly behind the batsman that is blank – it's pretty much impossible to hit a ball here:

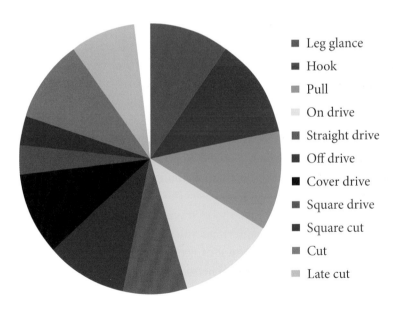

- Leg glance
- Hook
- Pull
- On drive
- Straight drive
- Off drive
- Cover drive
- Square drive
- Square cut
- Cut
- Late cut

Homework and kit maintenance

As a cricketer's family supporter you will have several responsibilities. The major one for all partners, wives and parents will probably be coping with the washing and cleaning of their kit.

Players need clean kit for every match. Sports teachers and club coaches have conspired over the years to ensure that those responsible for cleaning the kit have as little time as possible to do their work. They have a nasty habit of organising practices for the evening before a match, for instance. This means if your young player has only one set of kit and is a bowler or fielder who rubs the red ball on his trousers, or just a fielder who dives around on the grass and in the mud, you will need to get their kit washed and pressed overnight. This test of your ingenuity rapidly leads you to purchasing a spare set of kit (sometimes a secondhand set) which your player can use for practices, keeping his best set clean for the matches.

Years of cleaning muddy, grass-stained kit have given me several useful tips to share with you; I hope you find them useful.

Trousers, shirts etc.

Spray, coat or soak stains in a good proprietary stain remover (such as Vanish or Stain Devils) before washing the clothing in a medium-hot wash with a biological powder. This will result in most stains being removed from the white or cream cricketer's kit. Luckily most cricket kit these days is made from man-made fibre which washes and dries relatively rapidly. Metholated spirits used to be used to remove grass stains from cotton kit, but you should check if your player's kit is made from man-made fibres before using this.

Sports shoes

Since cricket shoes changed to being made of man-made material they have become much easier to maintain and, like trainers, can be popped into the washing machine with some stain remover and a biological detergent, though obviously you should remove any metal studs before you do this.

Alternatively, scrub them with a nail brush and some detergent, then rinse carefully. Always allow the shoes to dry naturally; never put them on a radiator as this will alter their shape. Stuffing them with newspaper while they dry can help. Finally, use some tennis shoe whitener to finish them off if there are still marks visible.

Sweaters

The majority of school sweaters are made from acrylic or cotton and are machine washable. They rarely pick up the same level of stains that the rest of your child's kit can experience and are therefore pretty easy to care for.

A word of warning: don't let a fond grandfather persuade you into using his treasured old woollen club or school sweater unless you're prepared to wash it by hand. One machine wash is likely to turn his pride and joy into a shrunken, matted sweater at least three sizes smaller than it was; machine washable wool is a relatively modern invention! This will not only annoy your small player who will not have a sweater to wear on what's likely to be the coldest day of the summer, but is likely to upset Granddad too.

Items like socks and box and pad shorts respond to all the same techniques that we suggest for other clothing.

Cricket Bats

As I explained earlier, you can't just buy a bat and use it straight away. It will need oiling and knocking in. You can of course get someone else to do it for you. Just take it to any cricket bat shop for treatment (though it might cost you a few pounds). You should also knock in your new cricket bat even if it comes advertised as ready to play, as it still won't be ready for the full force of a hard, new cricket ball, especially if you catch an edge or the ball hits the toe of the bat.

Firstly it needs oiling. Linseed oil is recommended (available from your bat shop) but note that it's best to avoid oiling your cricket bat if it already has an artificial coating (some bats are covered in a type of plastic coating). Never stand the bat in oil as this can cause the bat to soften and actually become more prone to damage.

It is always recommended that you knock in a bat, since this process hardens and knits the wooden fibres together and gives the bat a much greater punch. This helps the player to hit the ball better once the bat is exposed to a new cricket ball, which, as you are now aware, might be bowled at 90 mph by a good fast bowler. If the bat has not been knocked in enough, you will start to see seam marks on the bat.

You can get a special kind of rubber mallet to do the knocking in either online or from any bat specialist; see the links page for suppliers. However an old cricket ball inside a sock will work just as well. Whichever method you use be prepared to devote quite a long time to this process (about 5-6 hours of knocking is recommended) and you need to do it slowly.

If you are in USA or Canada and need to buy a bat mallet, you can find them at

>> http://shop.dreamcricket.com/dreamcricket/pavilion/pavhome.asp who are online suppliers to those countries.

The whole process will take several days, so do make sure you buy your bat at the start of the Easter holiday so it's ready for using at the beginning of term. Just follow these instructions:

Clean and clear the face of the bat, removing any face tape or fibre tape, and sand the face using fine sand paper. This makes the surface slightly rough to the touch.

Take about 7 or 8 drops of raw linseed oil in a piece of cloth (an old cotton hankie works well) and then wipe the face going from top to the toe. Do not oil around the splice area as oil could make the handle loose. Try not to over-oil either.

Once you've done the oiling, leave the bat laying on the ground horizontally, face up, for at least 24 hours. After that, push the face of the bat with your thumb. If you see the oil coming up on your thumb, leave it for another 24 hours. Assuming you have not over-oiled it, that should be plenty of time for the oiled wood to dry.

Now the knocking in. This will take a lot of patience on your part – be warned. Take your cricket mallet or an old high-quality leather cricket ball (for extra protection you should put it into an old sock), then start tapping. Tap the edges first and make sure to knock all the edges, even by the shoulders near the handle.

Once you've completed work on the edges, which will take 2-3 hours, you can start on the face of the bat. Again, just tap in the beginning. After a little while increase the intensity but make sure you avoid the splice area where the handle joins the blade. Be sure to knock the toe of the bat as well. You will note that you don't need to knock in the back of the bat.

By the end you should be hitting the bat with full force to simulate the impact of a real cricket ball. This is where the sock can help, allowing you to swing the ball hard into the bat.

Once you think the bat has gone through enough initial knocking, the player can start using the bat in the nets, but only with old balls. They should try not to catch any edges and should play the ball as straight as possible during this time.

After a day or two in the nets with old balls, they can start playing against new balls. If they feel jerks when the ball hits the bat, you will need to go back to knocking it in for a day more but now you can knock the bat hard.

Once the bat has been played in for a few hours in the nets it'll be ready to take out onto the square. It's a tedious process but well worth the time and effort for the results you get for your hard work.

After a match, a player should always check over his bat for signs of damage, such as cracking or splitting of the wood. Such damage can be repaired by sanding and cleaning the damaged area, then using super glue or cricket bat tape to repair any small surface cracks.

During the off season, avoid storing a new cricket bat in a dry, warm location. Particularly avoid storing a bat in direct sunlight or rooms in your house where there are artificially high temperatures, as this will definitely cause the bat to dry out. A dry garage or loft is a good storage area.

"So what does a bat do in winter?"   "It splits if you don't oil it, Sir"

At the end of the season if is often worth applying another light coat of linseed oil and again at the start of the next season. Just don't over-oil it or, you could end up weakening the willow.

If a player takes good care of his cricket bat it should easily last three to four seasons or more. However if he mistreats it and doesn't care for it, it will be much more prone to damage. It is normal though to get surface cracks on any cricket bat, even new bats, and as these are easily repaired with tape or glue, they shouldn't affect the quality of the bat. If a major split does occur it's worth contacting the supplier or shop where you bought it, as they may send it back to the manufacturer, who will often repair it or send you a new one. However if it is clear the bat has been mistreated, it's unlikely they will do so.

Other supporter roles

Cricket teas

Since the very first club cricket matches, the reputation of a club has rested on the quality of its tea as much as the cricket-playing ability of the team. So it is for schools today. The schools that can supply not just the players but also the spectators with an impressive afternoon tea will always be fondly remembered, and annual matches keenly anticipated.

Some schools are able to use their catering facilities to supply sandwiches and cakes, but other smaller establishments – and certainly most clubs – will have to rely on supporters to supply and make the tea. Favourites are cupcakes, strawberry, lemon and chocolate sponges and of course the ubiquitous cucumber sandwich. The boys will usually devour the cakes in preference to any sandwiches supplied, whilst the spectators often reverse this procedure.

Organising team cricket teas (including setting up rotas of helpers) can be a thankless task of course. If your youngster has volunteered you for this year's job try not to strangle them just yet!

It helps to have a list of home telephone numbers or parents' email addresses for all the members of the team, so that you can contact parents and persuade them to help. Remember there will always be one or two keen cricket watchers who can be relied on to turn up to most home matches. Make friends with these good souls and many of your problems will vanish since they will nearly always be there to help serve the tea, even if they have not helped to prepare the cakes and sandwiches.

If your cricket club has a tea urn, it's well worth getting to know how long it actually takes to heat up (sometimes many hours!), so you actually have hot water to make the tea at the right time.

Parents who cannot make it to the match can still usually be persuaded to bake or buy one cake a term and send it in with their son or daughter on the morning of a match. Games teachers are usually very amenable when it comes to collecting such offerings, but be wary of games masters with a sweet tooth or you may not have much cake left to offer guests by the time the tea interval occurs!

Hospital runs

Very occasionally a cricketer will get injured, although compared with some other sports, like rugby, injuries are very rare. Injuries that do occur include broken fingers (from catching speeding balls), broken toes (from wearing the wrong shoes against a fast bowler) and occasionally black eyes (if helmets are not being worn). So it's useful to know the location of the nearest A&E department to your cricket pitch. You can then run your small son or daughter straight there to get them checked out earlier than might otherwise be possible. I doubt you'll need to do this more than once, if at all, during your child's cricketing career, but as the Boy Scouts say, it's good to be prepared. Bear in mind that black eyes respond well to arnica (cream or pills) and a bag of frozen peas to cool the bruising, and are often worn with a degree of pride by young players.

A new supporter's essential equipment

As a cricketing supporter you will rapidly discover that you cannot just turn up to a match in your usual working clothes and expect to enjoy an afternoon in the sun. Regrettably, the British weather is no respecter of our national summer game and regularly sends wind, rain and even hail to interrupt proceedings. Other more clement countries may not suffer as we do in the UK but here is a list of items that every cricketing supporter will find useful and from which you can select your own favourites once you have watched a few matches.

A light-weight garden chair. Cricket pitches are usually equipped with a bench or two and some schools and most large clubs boast superb pavilions with balconies and viewing areas, but most schools won't have these facilities.

A blanket. The need for a blanket will become apparent within minutes of your first match. Cricket pitches are usually set in the middle of open spaces where the wind whistles through. The season starts in April in the UK, and that brings blustery showers and cool evenings.

An umbrella and waterproof jacket or poncho. The English spring or summer shower can easily turn into a downpour. Whilst some schools will have a pavilion in which you can shelter, some pitches are set a long way from the main 1st XI pitch and its pavilion or the school car park, and you may need to seek refuge from the rain without the benefit of a building to protect you.

A sleeping bag. If you can stand the inevitable teasing, this is the ideal form of protection from wind and weather. It will keep you warm, protect you from the rain (so long as it has a waterproof outer cover) and will ensure that you can watch an entire match in comfort whatever the weather.

A flask of hot tea or coffee. Not all schools are able to provide hot tea for visiting supporters (especially when pitches are a long way from the school buildings or pavilion). This can be very useful for staving off hypothermia!

Snacks or supper. Mid-week matches often finish around 7 o'clock in the evening and then there is a drive of anything up to two hours back home depending on the location of the opposition school or club team, and your own home's proximity to your child's school. If your child has homework to complete for school the next day, they will want to eat something on the journey, and although stopping for a burger or fish and chips might solve this problem, a bag of healthier snacks to keep hunger at bay until you reach home can prove extremely useful. They will have had tea after all.

Sensible shoes. Ladies, going to watch your child straight from work with your high heels and smart suit might seem a good idea on a lovely summer's day, but a pair of old flatties in your car boot just for walking to the cricket field will prove invaluable. The same goes for gentlemen who don't want to ruin their good office shoes – an old pair of shoes or trainers kept in the car will be really useful.

Supporter's etiquette

There are certain rules about being a good supporter that you should know before you come along to your first match. Most of them are simple common sense but if you're new to watching cricket I hope this breakdown will help.

Never walk around the pitch behind the bowler when he is in the process of bowling a ball. This distracts the batsman and is considered very bad form!

Obviously never sit or stand in front of the sight screen – it's there to make the batsman's job easier and allow him to see the ball. If you sit in front of it you will destroy this advantage and any movement you might make will distract the batsman when he needs to be concentrating on the ball heading in his direction. It might look like a perfect windbreak on a blustery spring or summer's day, but it's out of bounds for all good supporters.

Clapping both teams onto the pitch (and off at the end of the game) is good.

Clapping when a wicket is taken (whichever team is involved) is polite.

Clapping or cheering when four or six are scored is good.

Clapping when a no-ball is called would be bad.

Make sure you check the scoreboard regularly. It is traditional to applaud batsmen individually and collectively reaching 50 or 100 and multiples thereof. If the crowd suddenly starts applauding and you can't see a good reason for it, check the scoreboard and you might realise why.

In general, applauding good play and ignoring faults is the name of the game.

Balls can get lost around the edges of some cricket grounds and a good supporter will always help the fielding side find the ball as quickly as possible, regardless of which side is fielding. If nothing else it will speed up the game once the ball has been found.

If you have small children or a dog with you, do make sure you control them; there's nothing worse than interlopers on the field distracting the deep fielders. You may be tempted to speak to the fielder standing by the boundary – especially if it's your own son or daughter – but please don't. You should never distract them from their important role within the team.

Most Test match fielders standing near the boundary are happy to sign autographs during quiet moments in the match, but they only do this between overs or when the ball is out of play.

'Oh look, he's seen us'

As a good supporter you will never dispute the umpire's decision. Remember the Spirit of the Game precludes this for the players and you should be just as well behaved!

Obviously there are major differences for spectators attending school or village matches and going to a Test match. School and village matches are social events, people chatter away and can seem to be completely ignoring the game taking place whilst they have a good catch up with friends and family. At a small village ground this can seriously annoy the players and be very distracting. If you are having a conversation, please at least keep the volume down.

Remember it always helps to concentrate on the game as you never know when a boundary will be scored – and balls hit for six can land in the crowd. A spectator catching a ball gets great kudos, but getting hit on the head because you're not watching what's going on is somewhat embarrassing.

Do try not to nod off, you really don't want to miss a vital moment of the match involving your young player. What could be worse than being asked after the game 'Did you see my brilliant one-handed catch?' and then having to say 'Ooh, er . . . well, no sorry'.

At Test matches, happily, quiet conversations are the norm. There is a gentle buzz from a Test crowd, but in addition there will be occasional singing, chanting and on the Saturday of a Test match, dressing up in fancy dress is commonplace. You will see groups of Elvis impersonators, Marilyn Monroes, cartoon heroes and sexy nurses – and that's just the men! These have become traditional on this day's play. I am always amazed at the costumes some people wear – especially furry animal outfits which must make them very hot on a summer's day – but it's all part of the fun.

In addition various Test teams have traditional musical accompaniment: the West Indies have drummers and whistle blowers, England has a trumpeter who attends matches playing everything from the theme from *The Great Escape* to Colonel Bogie and the National Anthem for the crowd to sing along to. England's Barmy Army is a group of noisy and exuberant supporters who follow the Test team all over the world. They chant out to the opposition supporters during a match and have special chants or songs for members of the team whenever they come on to bowl or bat. Such behaviour will probably be frowned upon at a school match!

Young England player, Joe Root, has the unenviable support of a long Roooooooot being called out by the crowd whenever he comes onto the pitch or does something special (bowling or batting well). Sadly this sounds very much like a 'boo' coming from the crowd, so if you hear this during a match, don't be alarmed, they are supporting Joe, honestly.

Scoring

If you are beginning to develop a keen interest in this wonderful game and want to have something more interesting to do during an afternoon's match rather than just sitting on the boundary waiting for your youngster's turn to bat, why not learn how to score? You'll become very popular if you can do this and will escape other supporter duties, like making the tea! You will also, at many grounds, get the advantage of sitting in the scorers' hut or room, which means you're protected from whatever weather the rest of the spectators have to endure.

Each team has its own scorer, so you will get to meet other interested people if you take up this role. There are a couple of absolutely brilliant guides available online from these links (the pdf files are virus free currently):

>> http://media.wix.com/ugd/0ab80b_898aee1adeee4e9f82f382e92cf90ad8.pdf

and

>> http://www.blackcaps.co.nz/uploadGallery/umpires-and-scorers/Cricket_Scoring_getting_started.pdf

These give you just about everything you need to know about scoring and help you understand what's involved, but here's my brief analysis.

The scorer has four duties which are laid down in law 4 of the laws of cricket:

1. **Accept**
   The scorer may on occasion believe a signal from the umpire(s) to be incorrect but you must always accept and record the signals given. Remember the two scorers (one for each team) are part of a team of four and you must work together with the umpires.

2. **Acknowledge**

All umpire's signals must be acknowledged clearly and promptly; if necessary wave a piece of white card or paper if the umpires find you hard to see (remember you may be inside a scoring hut with the sun behind you). Confer with the umpires on any doubtful points when there are natural breaks in play (see point 4 below).

3. **Record**

Always write neatly and clearly – you'll see below how difficult this can be however!

4. **Check**

Do this frequently if you have any uncertainties.

Scoring equipment

The first and most important piece of equipment you'll need is a very fine nibbed pen. Score sheets are notorious for being far too small for their purpose and having fairy-sized writing skills will certainly help, along with the pen or a sharp pencil. In your early days of scoring it may be best to use a pencil which you can rub out as mistakes are easy to make. Then you can ink in the details afterwards removing the original pencil markings as you go. Some experienced scorers like to use different colour pens for different balls – red for no-balls for instance – or even different coloured pens for each bowler or batsman.

Other suggested items you'll be needing are:

▫ A copy of the local rules and the laws of cricket. In the UK this will be the 2000 Code 8th Edition including the 2013 updates.
▫ The team scorebook or an individual scoring sheet and a backing of stiff card or a clipboard.
▫ A clock or watch, a calculator (these are both readily available in a mobile phone nowadays), a pencil, a ruler, and an eraser.
▫ Clips (fold-back or paper clips are both useful on windy days).

- A spare notepad for calculations.
- Umbrella (bear in mind at some grounds there will be no cover available for you).
- Chair (ensure you have a comfy chair which is the right height for you to balance the scorebook and write easily).

At the start of the game, get someone to give you the names of all the players – not always easy – but your fellow scorer will know his or her own team's names and you will know yours, so you can usually work this out between you. Getting the list of batsmen in order of batting can be particularly problematic as at junior level teams will frequently change their minds about who to put in as the game progresses. This is another time when using a pencil initially is sensible.

If this has got you interested, just download the more detailed guide from the Sue Porter's Guide website:

» http://www.sueportersguide.com/page21.php.

Scoring can be great fun and it's a skill that will provide you with a hobby for life. I can certainly recommend it as a social activity.

Umpires' signals

In order for the scorer to be certain of what has happened after a ball is bowled, umpires have a set of special signals which they use to indicate specific events on the pitch. It's also useful for the spectator to know what these are.

I have already explained how the umpire shows that a batsman is out by raising his index finger, and further details of the frequently-used signals you will see during a match can be found on the following pages.

To indicate a wide ball he holds both arms out extended to the side and level with his shoulders.

To indicate a no-ball, he shouts loudly 'No-ball' and holds one arm only (normally his right arm) outstretched in the same way he would for a wide.

A bye is shown by one arm being raised above his head. For a leg bye the umpire taps on his thigh with his hand as well.

When four runs are scored the umpire waves one arm from side to side at waist level (frequently oscillating his hand as if indicating a bumpy sea).

For a six, he will raise both arms straight above his head. The great umpire Billy Bowden was famous for indicating sixes in a unique way, gradually raising his arms in triumphant steps until they were raised above his shoulders.

Four byes are indicated using a combination of the raised arm and the waving hand, while four leg byes obviously stretch the umpire's dexterity as he combines a four sign with a leg bye sign.

One solution is to slap his thigh with one hand and wave the other!

The umpire is also required to demonstrate to both teams when a new ball is about to be taken. Obviously this happens at the beginning of each innings, but in Test matches (and other matches that last more than a day) the new ball is made available every 80 overs unless it becomes damaged.

If a ball is damaged (the seam unravelling or it becomes too soft) a replacement can be requested. Balls that have been used in previous matches for a similar number of overs are then brought out for a replacement to be selected by the umpires.

In one-day matches each team generally starts its innings with a new ball. In addition, in one-day internationals, sometimes two balls are used, one from each end or the ball is automatically changed after around 35 overs have been completed.

In one-day matches when powerplay overs are used, the umpire will also demonstrate the start of a powerplay session by swinging his arm around like a windmill in front of him.

At the start of the over, the umpire also informs the facing batsman of the bowler's style of bowling (i.e. right-arm over) and finally, the umpire indicates the end of the over by calling out 'Over' so that the players (and hopefully the scorers) can hear.

The guide to scoring on the Sue Porter's Guide website gives a full list of the penalties and the runs that result from them, and the umpire will tap his shoulder to demonstrate that he's awarding penalties.

When the ICC are selecting international umpires they use the following criteria:

◦ Independent of the countries involved in the match or series
◦ The best available umpires for the match or series
◦ Better performing umpires used more often
◦ Frequency of individuals appointed to same teams
◦ Workload considerations

So you can see this is a serious matter for all concerned. Professional umpires have an interesting life visiting cricket playing countries around the world, although not everyone enjoys living out of a suitcase for most of the year.

I've already emphasised how important it is for the scorers to acknowledge all the umpires' signs, to show they have noted them correctly. Less experienced scorers sometimes forget this, since one hand will be holding the scorebook and the other will be busy writing down the details in three or four places on the page, and umpires frequently have to shout to make sure their signs are being acknowledged. If you see an umpire jumping up and down and waving his arms madly it's pretty certain he's trying to attract the scorers' attention.

The umpires not only indicate decisions to the scorers and spectators, but also act as coat hangers for the fielding team, wearing extra sweaters round their waists and clutching extra hats or sun glasses as and when required.

They have a tough job to do, standing still for long periods in what can often be quite cold conditions, and it is a wise umpire who learns the benefit of thermal underwear or an extra layers of sweaters early in the season when the spring winds blow and the benefit of wearing layers when the sweltering summer sun can make standing for several hours umpiring a game of cricket a difficult task. We can only imagine what life must have been like for an umpire of a ladies' match in the 1880's . . .

"Hope this women's game doesn't catch on .."

MCC spirit of cricket

I've already mentioned this development which resulted from the laws review in 2000, but here's the detail from the MCC themselves.

'The MCC remains responsible for the Laws of Cricket. However, it has long believed that the game should be played in accordance with its traditional "spirit", as well as within its Laws.'

In the late 1990s, two distinguished MCC members (and ex-England captains), Ted Dexter and Lord (Colin) Cowdrey, sought to enshrine the spirit of cricket in the game's laws. This would remind players of their responsibility for ensuring that cricket is always played in a truly sportsmanlike manner.

The Dexter/Cowdrey initiative proved successful. When the current code of laws was introduced, in 2000, it included, for the first time, a preamble on the spirit of cricket. As it says: 'Cricket is a game that owes much of its unique appeal to the fact that it should be played not only within its Laws but also within the Spirit of the Game. Any action which is seen to abuse this Spirit causes injury to the game itself.'

The preamble goes on to explain the roles and responsibilities of captains, players and umpires in respecting and upholding the spirit of cricket. Since the 2000 code was published, MCC has promoted the new laws – and the spirit of cricket – as widely as possible, both in Britain and overseas. As a result, cricketers, right across the world, are increasingly aware that they should not merely obey the game's laws but safeguard its spirit.

I was so taken with the spirit of cricket that I've included it in full here. If you can encourage your youngsters to follow this creed, they will turn into excellent players and sports people.

The Spirit of the Game

Cricket is a game that owes much of its unique appeal to the fact that it should be played not only within its Laws but also within the Spirit of the Game. Any action which is seen to abuse this spirit causes injury to the game itself. The major responsibility for ensuring the spirit of fair play rests with the captains.

Captains

There are two Laws which place the responsibility for the team's conduct firmly on the captain.

The captains are responsible at all times for ensuring that play is conducted within the Spirit of the Game as well as within the Laws.

Player's conduct

In the event of a player failing to comply with instructions by an umpire, or criticising by word or action the decisions of an umpire, or showing dissent, or generally behaving in a manner which might bring the game into disrepute, the umpire concerned shall in the first place report the matter to the other umpire and to the player's captain, and instruct the latter to take action.

Fair and unfair play

According to the Laws the umpires are the sole judges of fair and unfair play. The umpires may intervene at any time and it is the responsibility of the captain to take action where required.

The umpires are authorised to intervene in cases of:
◦ Time wasting
◦ Damaging the pitch
◦ Dangerous or unfair bowling

◦ Tampering with the ball
◦ Any other action that they consider to be unfair

The Spirit of the Game involves RESPECT for:
◦ Your opponents
◦ Your own captain and team
◦ The role of the umpires
◦ The game and its traditional values

It is against the Spirit of the Game:
◦ To dispute an umpire's decision by word, action or gesture
◦ To direct abusive language towards an opponent or umpire
◦ To indulge in cheating or any sharp practice, for instance:
  a) to appeal knowing that the batsman is not out
  b) to advance towards an umpire in an aggressive manner when appealing
  c) to seek to distract an opponent either verbally or by harassment with persistent clapping or unnecessary noise under the guise of enthusiasm and motivation of one's own side.

Violence

There is no place for any act of violence on the field of play.

Players

Captains and umpires together set the tone for the conduct of a cricket match. Every player is expected to make an important contribution to this.

Source: http://www.lords.org/mcc/mcc-spirit-of-cricket/what-is-mcc-spirit-of-cricket/spirit-of-cricket-preamble-to-the-laws/
© Marylebone Cricket Club

So there you have it, the Spirit of the Game in full. We're sure you'll approve of this initiative and hope it results in excellent sportsmanship right across the world of cricket for the foreseeable future. There are now Spirit of the Game ambassadors working around the world to ensure this happens. Britain's current ambassador is former England captain, Andrew Strauss.

International One-Day matches and powerplays

In July 2005, the International Cricket Council (ICC) announced changes to the way one-day cricket is played.

Before that time, for the first 15 overs, nine fielders, including the bowler and the wicket-keeper, had to be inside a 30-yard (27.5 m) circle when the ball was bowled.

The circle was marked out by markers five yards (4.5 m) apart, so the fielders – and umpires – knew where to stand (see our diagram on page 106 for example).

New rules from 2005 introduced the concept of power plays or powerplays, with the overall fielding restrictions being replaced by three blocks of play totalling 20 overs. Initially these were 10 mandatory overs at the start of the innings, then two further 5-over periods, one selected by the batting team and one by the fielding team.

The rules were amended in 2011 and again in December 2012. The October 2011 changes forced captains to take their powerplays between overs 16 and 40. This had the effect of preventing the fielding team from taking their powerplay immediately after the first 10-over period, which had become the norm.

In June 2015, in a move to give bowlers a bit of breathing room in 50-overs cricket, the ICC board decided to do away with catching fielders in the first ten overs, get rid of the batting powerplay and allow five fielders outside the 30-yard circle in the last ten overs of an ODI innings. The other notable change that took place from July 5 2015 saw free hits awarded for all no-balls in ODI and Twenty20 internationals, not just when bowlers overstep the crease

At all other times in a one-day international match, a maximum of four fielders are allowed to patrol the boundary at any time.

The changes also included an increase in the number of bouncers permitted in each over. Bowlers could now bowl two per over, doubling the previous limit.

The fielding powerplay period can only be invoked before the start of an over, and the umpire must be informed. The umpire will then signal the start of the fielding side's choice of powerplay by waving his arm round in a circular motion like a windmill sail.

Usually the fielding team will start with a third man and a fine leg in place to give the bowler protection on the off- and leg side.

With a brand new ball the bowlers should get movement from the ball, so you'll probably see a couple of slips and a gully in place to snap up those balls that get edged by the batsmen towards their direction.

The team's best and quickest fielders will often be at point and in the covers. Batsmen will be looking to drop the ball into any gaps for quick singles, so it's up to these two fielders to close down the space quickly and force run outs.

Placing a field during powerplays is definitely an art and a science and teams are very lucky if they have captains who excel at this.

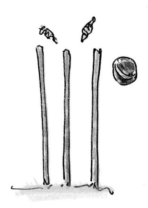

Duckworth-Lewis

One-day matches can be interrupted by bad weather, and when this happens, a highly complex calculation is made so that when a batting side returns to the pitch, the number of runs they need to beat their opponents is reduced in line with the number of overs remaining and in comparison with the score made by the first team batting.

You'll find the detailed charts at the end of the ECB section on Duckworth-Lewis, including the software needed to make the calculations.

This link will give you everything you need:

>> http://static.ecb.co.uk/files/2924-fc-duckworthlewis-2012-p365-378-lr-11946.pdf

If you just want a brief explanation, this is the text taken from the ECB website:

The D/L method sets revised targets in rain-interrupted limited-overs matches in accordance with the relative run scoring resources which are at the disposal of the two sides.

These are not in direct proportion to the number of overs available to be faced, as with the average run rate method of correction. Instead they depend on how many overs are to go and how many wickets are down when the interruptions occur.

To calculate the revised targets, you need to know the resources available at the stage of the match when suspensions and resumption of play occur. All possible values of resources have been pre-calculated and these are listed in the table. The table covers each individual ball in a game of up to 50 overs per side. The figures given in the table are percentages of the resources available for a complete 50-over innings.

For matches with less than 50 overs per innings before they start, the resource percentages available at the start of an innings will be less than 100%. But the same table and the same method of calculation are used whatever the number of overs per innings.

The single sheet over-by-over version of the table can be used for cases when play is suspended before the start of a new over.

When Team 2 (the side batting second) have less run scoring resources at their disposal than had Team 1 (the side batting first), their target is adjusted downwards using the ratio of the resources available to the two sides.

But when Team 1's innings has been interrupted, it often happens that Team 2 have more resources at their disposal than Team 1 had and it is now necessary to adjust Team 2's target upwards.

In the Professional Edition the target is adjusted upwards using the ratio of the resources available to the two sides.

In the Standard Edition the adjustment is based on the runs that would be expected to be scored on average from the extra resources at their disposal. The number of these extra runs required is calculated by applying the excess resource percentage to the average total score in a 50-over innings, referred to here as G50.

For matches involving ICC full member nations, including Under-19 international matches, or for matches between teams that play first class cricket, the value of G50 to be used at present is 245. For lower levels of the game, G50 should be chosen to represent the average score expected from the team. For matches between associate ICC members, for women's ODIs and for U15 internationals, the recommended value is 200. For other levels of the game, advice should be sought from the ICC.

So there you have it, a brief introduction to the Duckworth-Lewis method. You will almost certainly never need to use this system, unless you take up scoring as a career of course, but I thought it might help to know a little about how it works, to help you understand when TV coverage includes the D/L figure during a rain-interrupted match.

Useful links

Our own website, Sue Porter's Guides, which includes links to all our books and useful information such as scorecards and other downloadable files:
>> http://www.sueportersguide.com

Cricketing law and general information
A full edition of the current laws from the MCC:
>> http://www.lords.org/mcc/laws-of-cricket/laws/

The International Cricket Council's website which includes lots of information about international matches, both male and female:
>> http://www.icc-cricket.com/

The ICC development site:
>> http://www.iccacademy.net/

The England and Wales Cricket Board's website with information on matches, a fan zone and general information on cricket:
>> http://www.ecb.co.uk

UK first-class teams:
>> https://atheart.lv.com/sport/lv-county-championship-fixtures-2015

General information and news site:
>> http://www.itsonlycricket.com/

Disability cricket:
>> http://www.ecb.co.uk/development/club-cricket/
club-support/disability-cricket-at-your-club,3001,BP.
html%23photos=gallery_%252Fphoto-story.
html%253FLphotoId%253D1356866

England Minor Counties:
>> http://mcca.play-cricket.com/

A couple of alternative glossaries:
>> https://en.wikipedia.org/wiki/Glossary_of_cricket_terms
>> http://www.cricker.com/glossary/

Cricket History and Records

Wisden is the keeper of all cricketing records across the world – an invaluable resource for a cricket buff and fascinating for a newcomer to the game too:
>> http://www.bloomsbury.com/uk/special-interest/wisden/

There is also an excellent website for schools playing cricket which contains all sorts of useful information and results:
>> http://schoolscricketonline.co.uk/

The Lords website:
>> http://www.lords.org/history/mcc-history/

The new philosopher's stone which contains everything about anything:
>> https://en.wikipedia.org/wiki/History_of_cricket

This website includes a detailed glossary of all the common terms used in cricket:
>> www.cricker.com

Linked to the ESPN Sports TV station and all its cricket information:
>> http://www.espncricinfo.com/

The Times of India has a dedicated cricket website:
>> http://www.cricbuzz.com/

Sporteology:
>> http://sporteology.com/category/cricketeology/

Coaching and laws details

>> http://www.pitchvision.com/the-complete-guide-to-cricket#/
>> http://news.bbc.co.uk/sportacademy/hi/sa/cricket/skills/default.stm

>> http://www.pitchvision.com/cricket-show-20-how-to-stop-getting-out-lbw
>> http://www.cricketsecrets.com/
>> http://news.bbc.co.uk/sport1/hi/cricket/rules_and_equipment/default.stm

Spin-bowling coaching:
>> http://www.pitchvision.com/cricket-coaching/course/spin-bowling-tips/25/12#/

Bowling the flipper:
>> http://legspinbowling.blogspot.co.uk/2010/12/flipper.html

The substitution law I mention in the book:
>> http://www.rulesofcricket.co.uk/the_rules_of_cricket/the_rules_of_cricket_law_2.htm

Twenty20 cricket and other cricket variants

>> http://en.wikipedia.org/wiki/Twenty20
>> http://www.lastmanstands.com/
>> http://static.ecb.co.uk/files/kwik-cricket-rules-2014-12808.pdf

Kit

>> http://www.barringtonsports.com/cricket
>> http://www.discountcricketoutlet.com/
>> http://www.milletsports.co.uk/cricket/
>> http://www.seriouscricket.co.uk/
>> http://www.cricketdirect.co.uk/
>> http://www.3dsports.co.uk/
>> http://www.cricket-hockey.com/
>> https://romida.co.uk/
>> http://www.owzat-cricket.co.uk/
>> http://www.allroundercricket.com/

Bat care
>> http://www.middlepeg.com/cricketbatcare.htm
>> http://www.owzat-cricket.co.uk/acatalog/Cricket_Bat_Services.html
>> http://shop.dreamcricket.com/dreamcricket/pavilion/
pavdisplayproducts.asp?id=42&cat=Miscellaneous
>> http://www.cricketdirect.co.uk/catalogue/results.aspx?search=mallet

Girls' Cricket
>> http://ladytavernerscomps.play-cricket.com/

Scoring
>> http://media.wix.com/ugd/0ab80b_898aee1adeee4e9f82f382e92cf90
ad8.pdf
>> http://www.blackcaps.co.nz/uploadGallery/umpires-and-scorers/
Cricket_Scoring_getting_started.pdf

Kwik Cricket scorecards:
>> https://www.lords.org/assets/kwik-cricket-8-a-side-scoresheet
-10787.pdf
>> http://www.printablepaper.net/preview/Cricket_scoresheet

Duckworth-Lewis
>> http://static.ecb.co.uk/files/2924-fc-duckworthlewis-2012-p365-
378-lr-11946.pdf

Umpiring Guides
>> https://www.lords.org/assets/Uploads/olm-4th-edition-2010-4-10-
11-10712.pdf
>> http://www.cornwallcricket.co.nz/files/2364/files/Coaches/Cricket_
Umpiring_getting_started.pdf

and the same book from another New Zealand club
>> http://www.hamiltoncricket.co.nz/files/Cricket%20Umpiring%20
getting%20started.pdf

Afterthought

'It's a funny kind of month, October. For the really keen cricket fan it's when you discover that your wife left you in May!'

(Dennis Norden)

> George spent every Sunday playing cricket. It finally got too much for his wife, who exploded, 'Cricket! All you ever think about is cricket! I think I'd drop dead if you stayed home on a Sunday!'
>
> 'Now then, dear,' said George, 'it's no use trying to bribe me.'

Ladies, I sincerely hope I have been able to change the likelihood of either of these events happening in your life: that your interest in cricket has been kindled by this book and that you may be able to go along with your husband, boyfriend or partner and watch a match with renewed interest in future.

For my male readers, if you never played cricket yourself, I hope this will have given you an understanding of why your wife, partner or child is so keen on this game.

For everyone, at the very least I hope you will now understand a little more about what a keen cricketer, no matter what his or her age, is trying to do out there in the middle of that field all summer long.

If you've enjoyed this book, why not look out for our other guides:

Rugby Made Simple (**Published Sept 2015**)

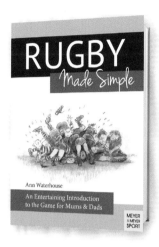

Football Made Simple (**Published Sept 2015**)

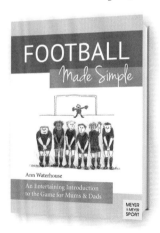

Don't forget you can check our website or more links and information on all these games:

» www.sueportersguide.com

Credits

Notes